LE MARCHE

an insider's guide

Peter Greene

Copyright © Peter Greene, 2013
All rights reserved

ISBN 978-1-4477-8199-8

www.le-marche.com
mail@le-marche.com

cover photograph: Cagli backstreet
© Huntley Hedworth

Contents

About the guide *7*

The essential Marche *10*

Background:

    Eating in the Marche *14*

    Wines of the Marche *19*

    Marche history notes *21*

    Significant dates *26*

    An art history sketch *27*

    Art masterpieces *30*

    The best buildings *33*

    Geography notes *34*

    Marche events *35*

Driving tours:

    Eight routes – an introduction *42*

    Tour 1 The lands of Montefeltro *43*

    Tour 2 In the footsteps of ancient Rome along the *via Flaminia* *46*

    Tour 3 From paper to stone – Fabriano, Monte Catria & its Valleys *49*

    Tour 4 The vineyards of Verdicchio *54*

    Tour 5 The heartland of the Marche *58*

    Tour 6 In the shadow of Monte Conero *63*

    Tour 7 The wild mountains of the Sibyl *67*

    Tour 8 Ascoli & Fermo's hidden heritage *71*

Beside the seaside – A Marche beach guide *76*

Places – an alphabetical gazetteer:

Ancona *82*	Corinaldo *89*
Ascoli Piceno *84*	Fabriano *90*
Cagli *85*	Fano *91*
Caldarola *86*	Fermo *92*
Camerino *87*	Fossombrone *93*
Cingoli *88*	Frassasi Caves *94*

Furlo Gorge *95*
Gabicce & Gradara Castle *96*
Jesi *97*
Loreto *99*
Macerata *100*
Monte Conero *102*
Offida *103*
Osimo *105*
Pergola *106*
Pesaro *107*
Piobbico & Apecchio *109*

Recanati *109*
San Benedetto del Tronto *111*
Sant'Angelo in Vado *112*
Sarnano *113*
Senigallia *114*
Serra San Quirico *115*
Sibillini Mountains *116*
Tolentino *117*
Urbania *118*
Urbino *119*
Visso *122*

Useful information & contacts

Getting to the Marche *126*
Getting around in the Marche *126*
Driving in the Marche *127*
Accommodation notes *128*
National holidays *129*
Language *129*
Weather *129*

Clothing *130*
Travel documents *130*
Tipping *130*
Medical matters *131*
Money *131*
Internet, phones & post *132*
Information resources *132*

Marche map *135*

Appendix 1: Italian-English menu translator *136*

Appendix 2: Notes if you're planning to move to the Marche

    Buying a house *138*
    Restoring property *139*
    Paperwork *140*
    Money matters *141*
    Health *141*

Index *143*

About the guide

For many central Italy embodies a certain type of perfect idyll - great art and architecture set against a sunny pastoral backdrop of olive, vine and cypress. But there is much more to the area than just the great cities of Florence and Siena, and the famous Tuscan countryside that lies between them. More independent travellers are now heading for the Marche, the easternmost region that makes up central Italy.

From being Italy's "best kept secret" – now a somewhat tired description - the Marche has become the new destination for travellers looking to find a more authentic version of Italy. Few areas of Europe offer such an alluring and unspoilt bucolic setting, a wealth of ancient historic towns, outstanding *cucina tipica*, and some fine beaches.

This book has been written by English guidebook writer Peter Greene, who has lived and worked in the region for more than twenty years and also runs the popular *Marche Voyager* website.

It opens with *The Essential Marche* - everything you really need to know in a few pages - and continues with background notes on food, wine, history, art, geography and events. It then offers nine detailed driving itineraries that highlight many of the region's hidden delights, followed by a gazetteer of the larger towns and places of particular interest to visitors. It closes with a detailed section with useful information – from driving to clothing and from health to weather, and includes resources for further guidance.

The book is designed to give an honest view of the beauty and variety on offer in this central Italian region and uses a concise style that avoids the purple prose so prevalent when writing about Italy. It assumes most visitors are here to relax, and offers just enough to inform, without swamping the reader - art history students may have to look elsewhere. Most importantly, it aims to be as reliable as possible and is kept regularly up-to-date by the author.

Given the wide range of accommodation resources now available on the web, and the subjective nature of such choices, the book does not attempt to list individual hotels or other types of lodgings, but does include a section with helpful suggestions on where to start searching.

The book includes outline maps for the eight itineraries and a simple map of the main places in the Marche. However, you will want a proper map to find your way around the backroads. Either buy a copy of the *Touring Club Italiano Atlante Stradale d'Italia – Centro*, with 1:200,000 scale maps for the whole of central Italy, or get the *Umbria e Marche* sheet on the same scale and also from the TCI in their regional maps series.

If you have any comments on the book, notice errors, or think something worthwhile has been overlooked please do email the author at mail@le-marche.com.

Peter Greene
Cagli, 2013

The essential Marche

The region lies on the eastern flank of central Italy, between the Adriatic Sea and the high Apennine mountains. "Marche" is pronounced "markay" with the accent on the first syllable, is plural (hence *Le*), and is sometimes known as "The Marches" in English, or "the Marche" – the style we've used in this book..

The Adriatic coast has been popular for its sun 'n sand for decades. But few venture far from the beaches. Inland, perhaps more so than anywhere else in central Italy, you will find mountain villages where time still runs slower. In the Marche, culture comes in easily digestible proportions, which is not to say that the quality - witness Urbino and Ascoli Piceno - is not of the very best. But perhaps the greatest attraction of the Marche is discovering beguiling small towns that haven't yet been done to death by a thousand guidebook writers.

Whether you want to admire masterpieces of Renaissance art and architecture, trek across wild mountains, haggle over the best of the catch in a Mediterranean fishing port, or laze on a beach, the Marche has enough to keep you busy for years. And you will rarely have to jostle with hoards of other foreign tourists.

Many visitors who come to the area are looking for a taste of authentic Italy, unsullied by mass tourism, yet welcoming to foreigners - if that's what you want, you won't be disappointed.

City sights

Of the Marche's main towns, **Urbino** is perhaps the most interesting for the traveller. This jewel of a Renaissance city remains little changed from the days when Duke Federico da Montefeltro set up his celebrated court here in the second half of the 15th century.

The provincial capital of **Ascoli Piceno** lies at the southern end of the Marche. This splendid old town warrants at very least an overnight stay. Its travertine-paved main square is one of the most beautiful in Italy and its streets some of the most elegant in the region.

The capital of the Marche is **Ancona**, a city with less obvious attractions for the tourist. Give it time, however, and you may find you enjoy the salty charm of this bustling sea port. It is also the Marche's main ferry port with boats to Croatia, Greece, Albania, Montenegro and Turkey.

Another of the region's provincial capitals, **Pesaro** is both an appealing seaside resort and a thriving commercial town. Good shops, fine beaches and great fish.

The dignified town of **Macerata** is best known for its annual open-air opera festival, but is worth a visit at any time of the year.

The alluring hill town of **Fermo** is the capital of the province of Fermo and boasts a fine historic centre and an imposing main *piazza*.

Smaller inland towns in the Marche that are well worth visiting or that might make a good base for touring include **Camerino, Cingoli, Cagli, Jesi, Recanati, Sarnano,** and **Tolentino**.

Of the many seaside resorts, the prettiest is **Sirolo** on the Conero peninsula, while other lively seaside towns include **Gabicce**, **Fano**, **Senigallia**, and **San Benedetto del Tronto**.

Natural born stars

Many tourists visit the Marche for their natural beauty and most of the spectacular inland mountain country remains relatively unscathed by the worst excesses of the past hundred years. Here are some of the major sights that should not to be missed:

The **Frasassi Caves** are some of the most spectacular limestone caverns in Europe.

Limestone again is the leading player at the **Furlo Gorge**, a dramatic natural pass through the mountains that has been a trading route since prehistoric times.

Most of Italy's Adriatic coastline is stubbornly flat. **Monte Conero**, just south of Ancona, is a rare exception - a limestone mountain that plunges into the sea and guards a handful of delightful bathing coves.

You'll find some of the Marche's most impressive mountain scenery to the south of the region amidst the **Monti Sibillini**, whose peaks are often covered with snow until late spring.

The best mountain views to be had in the north of the region, on the doorstep of Urbino, are around the giant **Monte Catria**. In spring the upland meadows are carpeted in alpine flowers.

Art matters

While it may not have the abundance – some might say excess – of great art treasures that you'll find in neighbouring Tuscany or Umbria, the region can take pride in some outstanding masterpieces by the likes of **Piero della Francesca, Raphael, Lorenzo Lotto** and **Carlo Crivelli**. See page 30 for a list of the most outstanding works.

Monumental marvels

Like the rest of central Italy, the Marche landscape is littered with the remains of its long history. Highlights include the Roman arches at Ancona and Fano, the amphitheatre at Urbisaglia, the Cathedral of San Ciriaco at Ancona, the romanesque church Santa Maria A Pie' di Chienti, the castle in the centre of Sassocorvaro, the main square in Ascoli Piceno, Jesi's *Palazzo della Signoria*, and Urbino's *Palazzo Ducale*. See page 33 for a list of the major monuments.

When to go

While it can be hot between late June to mid-August, it is rarely overcrowded and up in the hills the breezes are cooling.

May and September are the ideal months to tour the Marche if you prefer to keep cooler; the landscape is clothed in spring green or the first tints of autumn, any rain tends towards brief showers rather than endless drizzle, and it is usually possible to find a bed without booking to far in advance.

The wettest seasons are mid-February to early April and November to mid-December when days of mist and rain can set in. It can also get decidedly cold, particularly when the northerly *tramontana* wind blows. For more on the weather see page 129.

> **Note on opening times**
>
> Apart from a handful of museums and galleries that remain open all day – including Urbino's Palazzo Ducale - most close at lunchtime with only a few re-opening in the afternoon. Nearly all remain closed on Mondays but are open on Sundays.
>
> Churches often open only in the mornings and close promptly at 12.30pm; sometimes you will have to hunt out someone who holds the key to open up – rarely as hard as it might sound.
>
> Remember when visiting towns in the Marche - or anywhere else in Italy - that from lunchtime until around 4pm many places can seem like ghost towns. To see them at their liveliest try to arrive mid-morning, or late afternoon in time for the *passeggiata*, the ritual evening stroll.

Background

Eating in the Marche

Cooking in the Marche is deeply rooted in peasant tradition and remains impervious to the arrival of frozen *bastoncini di pesce* (fish fingers). Here the humble cook rather than the professional chef rules and even the smartest restaurants seek to produce food just like *nonna*, or grandmother, used to make.

The use of fresh, top-quality materials assembled with the minimum of fuss is a feature of central Italian food. But as dishes are strictly based on local produce and traditional tastes, each small area has its distinctive *cucina tipica*, with a strong sense of the seasons.

As with any rural diet, much use is made of food gathered from the wild; *funghi*, game, nuts, field herbs and truffles - the area's greatest culinary treasure - are an important feature.

Waste, too, is frowned upon, and many of the now most fashionable dishes were first developed to use up such things as stale bread or the less appealing parts of the pig.

Not surprisingly, the best food is still to be had in local homes rather than in restaurants. The arrival of tourists, however, has often raised the standards in restaurants and led to the "rediscovery" of long-lost traditional dishes.

Wild things

From springtime onwards people with over-stuffed carrier bags drift across fallow fields, studying the ground as they go, gathering the many wild herbs - *erbe del campo* - that still play a part in the *marchigiano* diet.

Weeds such as the common dandelion, field poppy and the more tender types of thistle are carefully cut at their roots to be eaten either raw in salads as a *misticanza*, or boiled before being quickly tossed in good olive oil with a clove of garlic and a squeeze of lemon juice at the end.

The hedgerows also have treasures; one of the most common climbers across Europe is wild clematis or old man's beard, *Clematis vitalba*. Here in the Marche it is know simply as *vitalba* and the young growing tips - roughly the first 10cms - are picked in spring. They are then blanched in boiling water for a few minutes to get rid of the excess bitterness before being added to a *frittata*, or Italian-style omelette.

The old labels *ristorante*, *trattoria* and *osteria* have become somewhat interchangeable in recent years; many of the smarter, and most expensive places, now call themselves *osterie* and take pride in reinterpreting local dishes with great flair. Many restaurants also double as a *pizzeria*, but note that pizzas are usually only available in the evening when the wood oven is fired.

Generally, though, a *ristorante* will have a written menu and a broader choice of wines. In *trattorie*, particularly in country areas where the menu changes each day,

CHALET BALOO - GROTTAMMARE
Country House IL GIRASOLE, MASSIGNANO

you will often have to cope with a menu rattled off at your table by the proprietor - at your blank looks a son or daughter with a smattering of English or French will be brought out from the back to assist.

Avoid the temptation just to order dishes whose names are familiar from back home - you will frequently be missing the best the house has to offer. If you are touring in summer or early autumn, look out for posters advertising the local *sagra* - a festival dedicated to a town's particular culinary speciality.

The menu

The *marchigiani* eat more meat than any other Italians according to official statistics, and in many country areas going out to a restaurant is an excuse to stoke up on platters of excellent quality, charcoal-grilled meats - *carne alla brace*. Relief from red meat, however, is on hand along the Adriatic coast with some of the Italian peninsula's best fish and seafood.

For an *antipasto*, mountain cured ham (the best is the *prosciutto di Carpegna*) and *lonza* (raw salted fillet of pork) reign supreme. Also try *ciauscolo*, finely-minced pork enriched with a generous amount of *pancetta*, or belly pork, which makes it soft and creamy; the most authentic versions come from Macerata province. In the Ascoli Piceno area, try *olive ascolane*, deep-fried stuffed olives, accompanied by *crema fritta*, cubes of deep-fried egg custard.

The classic *primo* is a generous plate of *tagliatelle* dressed with a *sugo*, or meat sauce. The region's unique pasta dish is *vincisgrassi*, a rich, baked lasagne (see page 61). Urbino is also famous for *passatelli*, strands of pasta made from breadcrumbs, parmesan cheese, and egg, cooked and served in broth. In season, try the region's greatest gastronomic triumph, a plain plate of spaghetti or risotto with abundant white truffle grated over it when served.

Apart from the ever-present meat grilled *alla brace*, on embers, delicious stuffed pigeon (*piccione ripieno*) and rabbit cooked with wild fennel (*coniglio in porchetta*) are Marche specialities. Also look out for young lamb (*agnello*) and *castrato*, more mature lamb, both excellent when plainly grilled.

By the coast try *brodetto*, fish stew which, according to purists, must be made with 13 species of fish, no more, no less (see page 112). At Ancona the dish to try is *stoccafisso all'anconetana*, prepared with dried cod. Thin spaghetti dressed with *vongole*, or baby clams, is always good as is spaghetti *allo scoglio*, "on the rocks" dressed with a variety of shellfish.

In the northern Marche look out for *piadina* or *crescia*, a flat, unleavened bread usually made with lard and often served with cold meats at roadside snack-bars. The ewe's milk *pecorino* cheese is excellent and is best eaten in the spring with young raw *fave*, or broad beans. Look out, too, for *formaggio di fossa* (a strong-flavoured cheese aged in underground pits).

Don't be afraid to order just a *primo* or *secondo* with maybe a salad or *contorno*, or vegetable, in a restaurant – many Italians do likewise.

On market day in the Marche make for the *porchetta* van to buy slices of a whole roasted boned pig stuffed with wild fennel, served in a chunky bread roll.

> **Eating everything but the squeal**
>
> In the bright frosty air of January the upland valleys of the Marche resound to the squeals of pigs as they face the butcher's knife in small farms across the region. The pig remains a central part of the traditional diet of the *marchigiani* and here everything does get used except for the squeal.
>
> Most of the carcass is salted to produce *prosciutto crudo, pancetta, lonza, salami* and sausages; the parts of the pig that need to be eaten fresh keep many a family going for a good few weeks.
>
> The head is used to produce *coppa di testa*, a type of brawn, and even the blood is kept to make a daunting dessert called *sanguinaccio*, a cross between chocolate mousse and black pudding. The best belly fat is minced and salted to make *lardo*, an essential ingredient in rich meat sauces used to dress pasta, while poorer fat is rendered down for *strutto*, or lard (note that Italian "*lardo*" is not "lard").

Food Shopping

The invasion of supermarket culture is fast changing the shopping habits of the *marchigiani*, but the small grocers, butchers, greengrocers and fishmongers of the typical Marche town have not yet disappeared. While they may not be able to compete on price with the big chains, they often offer better quality local produce.

Most food shops – apart from the large supermarkets – generally close for lunch, usually between 1pm and 4.30pm, and remain closed for one afternoon a week. On Sundays, only the *pasticcerie* (cake shops) and *pasta fresca* (fresh pasta shops) are open, although many supermarkets now have Sunday morning opening.

In most grocers' nowadays, the food is on the shelves for you to help yourself, except for the delicatessen counter, where you will often need to ask for bread. When ordering from the delicatessen counter, most things are sold in units of *etti* (*un'etto/due etti*) one *etto* = 100 grams, or slightly less than a quarter pound. For small quantities it is common to use a half *etto* (*un mezz'etto*).

The following wordlists may be of use:

cheese - *formaggio*
ewe's milk cheese (local)- *pecorino* (*nostrano*)
parmesan cheese (freshly grated)- *parmigiano* (*gratuggiato*)
milk (full/semi-skimmed) - *latte* (*intero/parzialmente scremato*)
fresh cream - *panna fresca* (there is no "single" or "double cream"). For something to go with a sweet *mascarpone* cream cheese is often best.
bread (wholewheat) - *pane* (*integrale*)(bought by the half kilo or kilo - *mezzo kilo/un kilo*)
cured, raw ham - *prosciutto crudo*
cooked ham - *prosciutto cotto*
olives - *olive*

At the *fruttivendolo*, or greengrocer's, which stocks according to season:

apples - mele
artichokes - carciofi
aubergines/eggplants - melanzane
bananas - banane
broad beans - fave
courgettes - zucchine
cucumber - cetriolo
fennel - finocchio
french beans - fagiolini
garlic - aglio
lemons - limoni
lettuce - insalata

melon - melone
nectarines - pesche noce
onions - cipolle
oranges - arance
peaches - pesche
peas - piselli
peppers - peperoni
potatoes - patate
rocket/arugula - rucola
tomatoes - pomodori
water melon - cocomero / anguria

At the *macelleria*, or butcher's, you'll find:

beef - manzo
chicken (breast) - pollo (petto)
guinea fowl - faraona
lamb - agnello
liver - fegato
mince (lean) - carne macinata
(prima scelta)

pigeon - piccione
pork - maiale
rabbit - coniglio
steak (beef/pork) - bistecca (di manzo / di maiale)
sausages - salsicce
turkey - tacchino

At the *pescivendolo*, or fishmonger's, you'll find:

anchovies - acciughe/alici
salt cod - baccalà
sea bass - branzino
squid - calamari
monkfish - coda di rospa
mussels - cozze
prawns/shrimps - gamberi/gamberetti
cod - merluzzo
gilt-head bream - orata
oysters - ostriche
perch - pesce persico

swordfish - pesce spada
octopus - polpo/polipo
turbot - rombo
salmon - salmone
cuttlefish - seppia
mackerel - sgombero
sole - sogliola
tuna/tunny - tonno
red mullet - triglia
trout - trota
salmon trout - trota salmonata
baby clams - vongole

see appendix I (page 136) for an Italian-English menu translator

17

Edible gold

Good truffles are, weight for weight, one of the world's most expensive foods. Luckily, however, a little goes a long way and in the Marche you can indulge in them without pawning the family silver.

Of some sixteen species of *tartufi* found in the area, only two are really worth hunting out - the *tartufo bianco* or white truffle (Tuber magnatum Pico) and the *tartufo nero pregiato* or black truffle (Tuber melanosporum Vitt.).

The white truffle is the finest as well as the costliest - *tartufi bianchi* can cost over £3,000 a kilo depending on quality and size. The black version comes at a more modest price. Both are a perfect antidote to the hard winter; to buy them fresh you have to be here between October and the end of December for the *bianchi* and between December and March for the *neri pregiati*.

In summer any fresh truffles to be found on restaurant menus will be the *tartufo d'estate* or summer truffle (Tuber aestivum Vitt.), a pale, though much cheaper, shadow of its noble sister.

Italian truffle hunters dig up over one hundred metric tonnes of truffles a year with the help of their often mongrel dogs. In the Marche, Acqualagna and Sant'Angelo in Vado are the places to head for during the late autumn & winter truffle season.

Although truffles are best eaten fresh within days of their discovery, there are plenty of products that try to preserve the experience. Best value are the small bottles of olive oil flavoured with truffles, but check they don't list *"aromi"* amongst their ingredients (shorthand for a rather heavy-handed artificial "truffle" flavouring). Other good buys are truffle butter and truffle paste. Chocolate "truffles" flavoured with real black truffle may sound bizarre put are curiously good.

The wines of the Marche

Wine alone could provide an excellent motive for touring the Marche and winemaking in the area has been having its own little Renaissance over the last decade or so, with a move away from quantity towards quality.

From producing rough plonk for the masses, the region now boast some outstanding *vini da meditazione*, wines so good they should be drunk with religious respect. These top flight wines are not cheap, but they are some of Italy's best and are difficult to find outside the region. Italy's wine and food magazine Gambero Rosso regularly features a growing number of Marche producers in its annual *Tre bicchieri* wine awards. But as well as the award-winning labels, you can drink excellent wines at reasonably low prices.

Joy, anyway, is not only to be found in the restrained sipping of august bottled vintages, but also in the quaffing of young, local wines. These still-living brews are liable to dramatic alteration at the mere changing of the moon, and are barely able to withstand the journey from cellar to table - let alone a long trip north - yet often delight by their incisive personality and honest price. Often - but, be warned, not always - you won't go far wrong simply sticking to the *vino della casa*.

Wine choices

Whites

The region's pride is **Verdicchio** made from the eponymous local grape. This green-tinged wine with a distinctive bitter finish goes well with the region's Adriatic fish. It is among Italy's best-known dry whites, and it has come a long way since the commercially successful but sometimes mediocre Verdicchio of a couple of decades ago. The two DOC (the official Italian equivalent of the French *Appellation Contrôllée*) versions are - **Verdicchio dei Castelli di Jesi** and **Verdicchio di Matelica**. The *Riserva* versions of both wines have been given the elite DOCG title. Other Marche DOC whites include **Bianchello del Metauro** and **Colli Pesaresi Bianco** from the north, **Esino Bianco** and **Colli Maceratesi** from the central Marche, and **Falerio**, and **Offida Pecorino** and **Passerina** from the south.

Reds

While the Marche is known world-wide for its white wine, the region also makes some outstanding reds. Around the Conero peninsula, **Rosso Conero**, made from the Montepulciano grape sometimes with a small amount of Sangiovese, is a rich, perfumed wine that occasionally reaches true greatness. The *Riserva* version has now been given DOCG status. **Rosso Piceno**, and the even better **Rosso Piceno *Superiore*** from the central and southern Marche, blend Montepulciano and Sangiovese grapes. A sparkling oddity is **Vernaccia di Serrapetrona**, normally a sweet red dessert wine but also available in a drier *secco* version. Marche DOC reds include **Sangiovese dei Colli Pesaresi** around Pesaro, **Pergola Rosso** from the eponymous town in Pesaro & Urbino province, **Esino Rosso**, and the intensely-scented **Lacrima di Morro d'Alba**, both from the central Marche, and **Offida Rosso** from the south.

Other drinks

Wild sour cherries, or *visciole*, are used to make a lip-smackingly delicious liqueur in the northern Marche called **visner** or **vino di visciole**. This *digestivo* is made by macerating the crushed dark cherries in red wine with sugar and other ingredients. For the very best you really need to try the home brews made using secret family recipes passed down from generation to generation, but a number of local producers now make excellent commercial versions for sale in *enoteche*, or wine shops, across the region.

When *marchigiani* take their coffee *corretto* - with an added shot of liquor - it is likely to be with **mistrà**, the aniseed flavoured liqueur most characteristic of the region. As well as being drunk in coffee or straight as a *digestivo* after a meal, it is also used to add the finishing touch to the Marche speciality *coniglio in porchetta*, or rabbit cooked with wild fennel. The most noted brands are **Varnelli** and **Meletti**.

Vino cotto (or **vin cotto**) is a sublime dessert wine from the south of the region made by boiling down fresh grape must in copper cauldrons - hence *cotto* or "cooked". The reduced must is poured into small oak barrels that already contain a quantity of *vino cotto* from the previous year and left to ferment slowly. The high sugar level produces an alcohol content of around 14%. As well as being an excellent *digestivo*, it marries well with *ciauscolo*, the soft *salame* from the area. The "capital" of *vino cotto* in the Marche is the village of Loro Piceno in Macerata province which dedicates an annual *sagra* to the brew in August.

Vino santo (or **vin santo**) is made across central Italy from grapes left to dry before being slowly fermented, the high sugar content producing a strongly alcoholic dessert wine. Sant'Angelo in Vado in the north and Offida in the south are towns particularly noted in the region for this heavenly sweet wine.

Sugar was once an expensive commodity in Italy and, along with honey, the people of the Marche used concentrated grape must, or **sapa**, as an alternative. The thick, dark syrup is still made by slowly boiling white or red grape juice until it is reduced down by about two-thirds before being bottled. Its intense caramel and honey savour with a faintly sour edge is surprisingly versatile, is not dissimilar to good balsamic vinegar, and works well with strong cheeses and simple grilled meat, or as a topping for ice cream and *panna cotta*.

Marche history notes

Few areas in the world are infused with such a strong sense of historical continuity as central Italy. From the myths that surround the birth of Rome to the unification of Italy in the 19th century, past and present are inextricably linked in a narrative that stretches back over three millennia.

This short account provides a thread to guide you through the labyrinth of this complex story and focuses on the currents of history that most affected the Marche.

Before the Romans

Our knowledge of the early peoples of the Marche is hazy and often draws on the unreliable writings of later, often biased, Roman historians. The most important of the tribes who first inhabited the region in any numbers were the **Piceni**, who lived on the eastern seaboard of the Marche. Up in the mountains to the north their place was taken by the **Umbri** tribes who also dwelt in the neighbouring region now know as Umbria. Neither tribes have left us many relics of their passage.

There are various theories about the origins of the *Piceni* who settled the area between the 9th and 10th centuries BC. Some suggest that they came from the Balkans, arriving by sea, while others maintain that they were a group of Sabines from Marsica who, tradition recounts, were guided here by a woodpecker (*picchio* in Italian), today the official symbol of the regional authority.

Ancient Rome

With the expulsion in 509 BC of the last of the Etruscan Roman kings, the new **Republic of Rome** gradually began to make its presence felt. Already weakened by attacks from the Greek colonists in southern Italy – who founded **Ancona** around 387 BC - and by Celtic inroads from the north – a group of Gallic celts known as the Senones founded **Senigallia** in the 4th century BC - the Piceni and Umbri soon came under the sway of Rome.

The ancient Roman legions final overcame their arch-enemies, the Carthaginians - and killed Hannibal's brother Hasdrubal - at the **Battle of the Metaurus** in 207 BC near the modern-day Metauro river in the northern Marche.

With the construction of the great highways such as the **Via Flaminia** (in 220 BC) and the older **Via Salaria**, Roman dominion across Italy was consolidated. Under the first Roman Emperor, **Augustus** (63 BC to AD 14), the Marche was divided - the northern stretches formed part of Roman **Umbria**, while the south was known as **Picenum**.

21

Arrival of the Barbarians

In AD 476, Rome - already weakened by the split between the **Western and Eastern Empires** and the first forays by **Goths** and **Vandals** from the north - finally fell to the barbarian warrior **Odoacer**. His reign as the first King of Italy was short-lived, however, with the arrival in 489 of **Theodoric**, King of the Ostrogoths, who established a 33-year rule of relative tranquillity in Italy.

On Theodoric's death, the Eastern Roman Emperor **Justinian** in Constantinople tried to revive Byzantine imperial power in Italy through his celebrated generals **Belisarius** and **Narses**. Although they finally managed to topple the Gothic King **Totila** in 552 when the deciding battle took place at the **Furlo Gorge** in the Marche, central Italy was unable to resist yet another invasion from the north, this time from the **Lombards** in 568.

For two hundred years these warriors from the Danube valley held loose control over much of central Italy, ruling from Lucca and Spoleto. Only in the northern Marche and part of Umbria did the **Byzantine** powers manage to keep a toe-hold under the protection of the **Exarchate of Ravenna**. One of the key possessions of the Exarchate was the the medieval **Pentapolis**, or grouping of five cities made up of Rimini (now in neighbouring Emilia-Romagna), Pesaro, Fano, Senigallia and Ancona.

Why "Le Marche"?

Territories which lay on the borders of the Holy Roman Empire in medieval times were know as "marches" from the German *marka*, and the governor appointed to rule such lands was known as a *markgraf*, hence the English word "marquess". *Le Marche* is the plural form of the Italianized *la marca*, and referred to the *marca*, or march, of Ancona and the nearby *marche* of Camerino and Fermo.

The Holy Roman Empire

The Lombards were converted to Christianity by Pope Gregory the Great, but were regarded as unwelcome guests by later popes. It was Pope Stephen II who first hit on the idea of calling in foreign help to oust the Lombards and in 754 **Pepin the Short** entered Italy at the head of his **Frankish** army. The expulsion of the Lombards proved difficult and it was only under Pepin's son, the great **Charlemagne**, that the work was completed.

As a reward to his Frankish champion, Pope Leo III crowned Charlemagne as the first **Holy Roman Emperor** on Christmas day 800. Although at the time it was little more than an honorary title, the Holy Roman Empire, once founded, was to continue, with the odd break, for a thousand years, and to become the focus of continual strife between the rival claims of successive popes and emperors.

Although Charlemagne's empire flourished, it depended too heavily on his guiding hand and when he died in 814 things rapidly fell apart.

Italy was again plunged into anarchy with imperial officials setting themselves up as local despots. Increased security only returned with the revival of the Holy Roman Empire under the Saxon King, **Otto I**, crowned Holy Roman Emperor in 962. Trade and industry began to flourish and, while Emperor and Pope argued over who should rule, many of the cities of central Italy, the Marche included, had their first taste of independence. Although they paid lip service to one side or the other, in truth they found themselves able to decide their own future. Bereft of effective central government, these early city states bred fierce local patriotism and ceaseless rivalry with their neighbours, distinct traces of which still remain today.

Guelphs & Ghibellines

The rivalry between the Papacy and the Holy Roman Empire came to a head under the rule of the brilliant medieval German Hohenstaufen Emperor, **Frederick II**, the man who earned the title *Stupor Mundi* for his dazzling talents. If you visit **Jesi**, you'll be able to see the square where he was born in a tent on 26 December 1194 - some chronicles claim that his mother gave birth to him in a public place to forestall any doubts about his origins. Although he almost succeeded in unifying Italy, his death in 1250 marked the eclipse of German imperial power in the peninsular.

The Marche, like the rest of central Italy, was deeply bound up in the conflict between the **Guelph** and **Ghibelline** factions. The Guelphs, supporters of the papacy, took their name from Frederick's rival for the empire, the Welf Otto, while the imperialists became known as Ghibellines from the Italianised Hohenstaufen battle-cry *Hie Weibling*.

Behind the simple struggle between the two powers lay a deeper political battle between the new middle-class of merchants and artisans, who allied themselves with the Guelphs, and the old feudal aristocracy who saw that the dangerous tide of democracy could best be held back by the Emperor's Ghibelline faction. Into this fundamental struggle all the warring factions of central Italy poured their energies. The Guelph cause can be said to have triumphed with the arrival of the French under **Charles of Anjou** in the middle of the 13th century at the invitation of Pope Urban IV. From now on, France rather than Germany was to be the dominant foreign power in Italy. The Guelph and Ghibelline labels, however, lingered on for centuries. Long after they had lost their original significance, they remained as a cover for just about any difference of opinion, or simply as an excuse to settle old scores.

Despots and republics

Autocratic rule by local despots flowered across the Marche in the fertile soil provided by the absence of the papacy from Rome while in **Avignon** in France from 1305-77, the subsequent **Great Schism** which saw up to three rivals claiming the papal throne, and the arrival of the devastating plague know as the

23

Black Death in 1348. Such families as the **Montefeltro** at Urbino, the **Malatesta** at Fano and the **Da Varano** at Camerino ruled with an iron will. The careers of these small-time tyrants were briefly interrupted by the arrival of the ruthless **Cardinal Albornoz**, sent by the Avignon popes to re-impose their rule over the Papal States, and they finally went into decline with the restoration of the papacy in Rome in 1421 under the strong Pope **Martin V**.

Peace before the storm

The apogee of the **Renaissance** in the middle of the 15th century was marked by a period of relative stability across central Italy. This was in no small part thanks to the **Italian League**, a defensive treaty between the major powers in Italy that held in check both the lesser Italian states and foreign invaders. It is against this background that many centres of art and learning flourished –the court founded by **Duke Federico da Montefeltro** at **Urbino** in the Marche was one of the most splendid.

Foreign domination and the Papal States

But the days of this prototype of an almost united Italy were numbered. The individual interests of the leading states soon took priority over the common good, and the arrival of **Charles VIII** from France in 1494, at the invitation of Milan in their quarrel with Naples, marked the dissolution of the League and the opening gambit in the **Wars of Italy**. Although the French invasion convulsed central Italy, two years later Charles was back in France with his Italian conquests lost.

But the French intervention had turned the thoughts of another great European power towards Italian conquests - **Spain**. As the 16th century dawned and the Italian Renaissance took root across Europe, central Italy along with the rest of the peninsular became a battleground on which the rival claims to Italian hegemony between **Francis I of France** and **Charles V of Spain** were tested. The signing of the Treaty of **Cateau-Cambrésis** in 1559 marked the start of over a hundred and fifty years of Spanish domination of Italy.

With the catholic Spanish holding the rest of Italy in check, the **papacy** was left free to consolidate its rule over its own possessions which included the Marche; while the centre of Italian culture moved to Counter-Reformation Rome, the Papal States were left to languish under the rule of the clergy.

Napoleon & The *Risorgimento*

The shock waves of the French Revolution of 1789 were felt in Italy and helped to fan the first flames of libertarianism that were to culminate in 1860 with the birth of unified Italy. But first it had to submit to the **Napoleonic invasion** of 1796. Across Italy, Bonaparte first set up client republics - with the Papal States transformed into the **Roman Republic** - then the more draconian **Kingdom of Italy**. Napoleon, in the wake of his successful invasion of the Papal

States, forced Pope **Pius VI** to sign away his possessions at the Marche town of **Tolentino** on 19 February 1797.

The collapse of the regime with the fall of Napoleon was as rapid as its arrival. But, despite its brevity, Napoleonic rule roused Italy from its long slumbers and was midwife to the birth of nationalism. Under the Piedmont **King Victor Emmanuel**, his wily prime minister **Cavour,** and the heroic if maverick general **Garibaldi**, a unified Italy became a reality. In 1859 the Italian tricolour flew from the Fortezza of Florence and the last Grand Duke, Leopold II, abdicated. A year later large parts of Italy opted to join the new Kingdom of Piedmont. The Papacy, however, proved more intransigent to the onslaught of the **Risorgimento**, or Unification of Italy, and it was only by force that the Marche managed to break free from the Papal States in the same year. One of the most significant battles between Victor Emmanuel's troops and the papal army took place at **Castelfidardo** near Ancona in 1860 when almost 90 soldiers lost their lives. It was a full ten years later that Rome itself finally fell, in 1870.

Significant dates

20,000-19,000 BC - Palaeolithic finds on Monte Conero; earliest evidence of habitation in the region.
7th-3rd centuries BC - *Piceni* tribes settle the Marche seaboard while the *Umbri* set up home in the mountains to the north.
circa 387 BC – Greek settlers from Syracuse in Sicily establish Ancona
295 BC - Battle of *Sentinum*; first victory for Rome in the region followed by the building of the first Roman colony at *Sena Gallica*.
207 BC - Roman legions kill Hasdrubal at the Battle of the Metaurus.
220 BC - Romans begin building the *Via Flaminia* - together with the *Via Salaria* in the southern Marche, it forms part of their great network of roads across Europe.
27 BC – AD 14 - Emperor Augustus reorganises the Roman Empire; the area of the southern Marche becomes the *Picenum* region while the north and west becomes Roman *Umbria*.
AD 476 - Rome falls to Odoacer and his barbarian warriors.
489 - the Ostrogoth King Theodoric topples Odoacer and begins his 33-year rule over Italy.
552 – Theoderic's successor Totila defeated near the Furlo Gorge by the Byzantine generals Belisarius and Narses in their campaign to reclaim Italy for the Eastern Roman Emperor Justinian.
568 - Lombard invaders arrive in Central Italy and bring Roman rule from Constantinople to an end. Only in the northern Marche does the Eastern Empire still hold power through the Exarchate of Ravenna.
754 - Pepin the Short and his Frankish army enter Italy at the invitation of Pope Stephen II and begin to oust the Lombards from their strongholds.
800 - Charlemagne, Pepin's son, crowned the first Holy Roman Emperor having successfully broken Lombard rule. Later he donates much of the Marche to the Papacy.
814 - Charlemagne dies and central Italy descends once more into anarchy.
1194 - Frederick II born at Jesi. His rule from 1215-50 as Holy Roman Emperor almost succeeds in creating a unified Italian state.
1200-1300s - Guelph and Ghibelline rivalry splits central Italy
1305-77 - Papacy moves to Avignon. Local despotism that ensues in central Italy is only quelled by the arrival of the ruthless Cardinal Albornoz in 1356.
1422 - Federico da Montefeltro born. The shining court he will create at Urbino becomes a Renaissance model of learning and art.
1559 - 150 years of Spanish domination begins in Italy leaving the Papacy free to consolidate its rule over its possessions in the Marche.
1796 - Napoleon invades Italy. Treaty signed at the Marche town of Tolentino in 1797 forces Pope Pius VI to sign away the Papal States.
1860 - Papal forces routed by the Piedmont army at the battle of Castelfidardo near Ancona in the fight for the Unification of Italy - the Marche region becomes part of the new Kingdom of Italy.

An art history sketch

The great cultural revolution known as the Italian Renaissance was born in central Italy and the Marche has its fair share of masterpieces by the leading artists of the period. Plain lists of painters and their works, however, often leave visitors confused, so here we give you a brief sketch of the history behind the masterpieces.

The Middle Ages

In the early Middle Ages following the collapse of Rome, between the 5th and 10th centuries, the people of the Marche were too busy with foreign invaders to bother much with the finer points of art or architecture. The few churches and monasteries that remain from this period tend to be in the oriental **Byzantine** style with eclectic touches from more "barbarian" cultures.

Only with the increasing wealth and stability of the late medieval period in the 11th and 12th centuries, did building fever really begin. The **romanesque** style of these years was both the sum of these new influences and a harking back to distant memories of Roman architecture.

As the romanesque was reaching its peak in central Italy, northern Europe was being gripped by the construction of the great **gothic** cathedrals. The solid walls and squat round arches of romanesque were being swept away by soaring pointed arches and flying buttresses that allowed walls to become frames for glittering panes of stained glass. The "gothic" label, though, was invented by Renaissance Italians as a term of abuse for a style they thought so barbaric it could well have been created by the savage Goths.

For all that, it was a potent influence in central Italy and in the Marche it was to have a strong influence on many of the great civic buildings of the 12th and 13th centuries. gothic architecture, too, was the stimulus for a revival in the arts of sculpture and painting; while Giotto's great frescoes and Nicola and Giovanni Pisano's sculptures were some of the earliest works to break free from medieval two-dimensional formalism, they were firmly planted in the gothic tradition. It proved a vigorous style that was to run through the early Renaissance. Its culmination came in the 14th century with the **International Gothic** school whose leading exponent was an artist from the Marche, **Gentile da Fabriano**.

The Renaissance

The great cultural revolution we call the *Renaissance* was not merely a school of painting, a style of sculpture or an architectural fashion, but an entirely new way of seeing the world. Remember that the Renaissance is a catch-all term describing over two centuries of human endeavour.

It was Giorgio Vasari who first drew together all the strands that ran through this great creative flowering in central Italy. In his *Lives of the Artists*, a collection of well-informed biographies of the protagonists of the Renaissance published in its final form in 1568, he characterised a period of some 200 years, from Giotto to Michelangelo, as a *Rinascita*, or rebirth, of art and architecture.

But it was not until the 19th century that the French word **Renaissance** was used to describe a whole period, set apart from what had come before. And it was with Jacob Burckhardt's *The Civilisation of the Renaissance in Italy*, published in 1860, that Italy was identified as the progenitor of a chapter in human history that still conditions much of Western perception of the modern world.

What Burckhardt saw as the key to the period was the growth of individualism - where medieval man had been content to work in collective anonymity to the greater glory of God, his Renaissance counterpart was much more interested in his own greater glory. Fame or notoriety - it mattered little which - became the goal, and competitive talent was all.

As if to wipe out the nightmare of the barbarian invaders, poets and painters, sculptors and scholars, looked to Ancient Rome and Greece as the source of all nobility and wisdom, and paganism and Christianity uneasily shared the same bed. Humanism released thought from the strait-jacket of medieval superstition while wealthy patronage fostered the cult of personality.

With human self-awareness came a new interest in the natural world, and artists turned to anatomy and mathematics with as much gusto as they did to the ancient world. The organisation of society, too, became a work of art, both in theory, as in Machiavelli's writings, and in practise, as in the glittering court of **Urbino**.

No longer was it adequate for the ambitious to be competent in one chosen craft, for the new age called for the master of many talents, the all-round Universal Man, epitomised by that peerless genius, Leonardo da Vinci.

The cradle of this revolution was **Florence**; its two great sons, **Dante** and **Giotto**, were born within a year of each other in the 1260s and with them we hear the opening bars of the overture. But the curtain was not to go up on the Renaissance until a hundred years later with the entry of that great Florentine trio, **Masaccio**, **Donatello**, and **Brunelleschi**, in the first half of the 15th century. Although he died in his late twenties, Masaccio (1401-c.1428) managed to revolutionise art with the first controlled use of perspective in painting and the introduction of full-blown humanism in the realistic portrayal of human suffering.

Sculpture, because of the ease with which it could realistically render the three-dimensional human form, was the greatest art of the age, and Masaccio's solid figures owe a great debt to the most celebrated of Early Renaissance sculptors, Donatello (1386-1466). Regarded by Vasari as equal to the sculptors of classical times, his incisive and emotive realism and sheer versatility have rarely been matched.

Both artists were profoundly influenced by the geometric principles of perspective laid down by Filippo Brunelleschi (1377-1446), the leading architect of his day. He is best remembered for the dome of Florence cathedral, a revolutionary feat of structural engineering, and his creative rediscovery of the *all'antica* vocabulary of the architecture of Ancient Rome.

During the course of the *quattrocento*, as Italians refer to the 1400s, numerous artists and architects perfected the achievements of the Early Renaissance - in

Urbino both **Paolo Uccello** and **Piero della Francesca** pushed forward the history of Western art with their pioneering exploration of foreshortening and perspective. In the Marche the leading architect was **Francesco di Giorgio Martini**, the man who masterminded impressive military complexes for **Duke Federico da Montefeltro**. Other great artists working in the Marche included the Venetian-born painters **Carlo Crivelli** and **Lorenzo Lotto**, both of whom have left many examples of their work in the region.

But it was the first half of the 16th century that saw the apotheosis of the Renaissance ideal of perfect beauty and harmony with the works of Leonardo, Michelangelo and the Marche's own **Raphael**, who was born in Urbino.

Mannerism and Beyond

A term that art historians love to argue over, **mannerism** loosely refers to Italian art between around 1520 and 1600. It was Michelangelo himself whom many regard as its creator. It is characterised by dramatic use of colour, distorted figures, violent compositions and a move towards the grotesque and outrageous.

For some it marks the triumph of style over content, an empty virtuosity for its own sake; for others, it is an assertive and intellectual breaking-free from the, by now, suffocating restrictions of classical Renaissance art. Its leading central Italian exponents include the painters Rosso Fiorentino, Pontormo and Bronzino, and the sculptors Cellini and Ammannati. In the Marche the style's greatest masters were **Federico Barocci** in Urbino and **Simone de Magistris** in Caldarola.

Whether or not we take to this highly subjective style, its liberation from the mathematical precision of Renaissance perspective and the confines of the block of marble paved the way for the great counter-reformation artistic movement of the 17th century that we call the baroque.

The region's best-known baroque painter was **Giovanni Battista Salvi**, better known as **Il Sassoferrato**, after the town where he was born in 1609 in the northern Marche. His glowing, devotional portraits of the Madonna were highly popular in the 19th century.

With the 17th century the central Italian age of artistic glory drew to an end; it is to other places and other nations that we must turn to follow the narrative of Western art and architecture.

Art masterpieces

The Marche region has numerous works by many of the great artists of the Italian Renaissance. Here are some of the best collections and individual works:

Ancona – Pinacoteca civica – Carlo Crivelli's *Madonna and Child*, Titian's *Virgin with Child and Saints*, and Lorenzo Lotto's *Sacra Conversazione*.

Arcevia – Church of San Medardo – two remarkable works (1507-08) by Luca Signorelli, and a terracotta altarpiece by Giovanni della Robbia (1513).

Ascoli Piceno – Duomo (Cappella del Sacramento) – a polyptych *of Madonna and Child with Saints,* regarded as one of Carlo Crivelli's finest works.

Ascoli Piceno – Pinacoteca Civica – two triptychs of *Madonna and Child with saints* by Carlo Crivelli and a 13th century cope (*piviale*) of Pope Nicholas IV, a dazzling piece of embroidery work made in England.

Jesi – Pinacoteca Comunale – some of Lorenzo Lotto's finest works, including *The Judgement of Santa Lucia*, a *Visitation*, an *Annunciation* and a *Deposition*, in a remarkable Rococo palazzo.

Loreto – the sanctuary of the Holy House includes frescoes by Melozzo da Forlì, and Luca Signorelli while there is a fine group of late works by Lotto in the Museo-Pinacoteca

Monte San Giusto – (SE of Macerata) Church of Santa Maria in Telusiano – Stirring *Crucifixion* by Lorenzo Lotto

Pesaro – Musei Civici – Giovanni Bellini's magnificent *Coronation of the Virgin*

Recanati – Villa Colloredo-Mels – a fine 18th century villa with four of Lorenzo Lotto's finest pictures, including a haunting *Annunciation*.

Tolentino – Basilica di San Nicola – Pietro da Rimini's grandiose Giottoesque frescoes in the gothic *Cappellone di San Nicola,* vivid masterpieces of the 14th century.

Urbino – Palazzo Ducale – includes Piero della Francesca's *Flagellation of Christ*, and *Madonna di Senigallia*, Raphael's *La Muta* and the famous vision of *The Ideal City* of uncertain attribution (possibly either Luciano Laurana or Piero della Francesca).

The Gothic Fantasies of Carlo Crivelli

Carlo Crivelli's work has been described as one of the major achievements of Northern Italian art in the *quattrocento*, or 1400s, and many of his paintings can be seen in the Marche, several still in the churches for which they were originally painted.

Crivelli was born in Venice around 1435, and among his early influences was Mantegna, the Renaissance master from near Padua. His career in Venice faltered in 1457 when he was convicted of adultery and sent to prison. After that it seems he left Venice for good, although he continued to sign himself "Caroli Crivelli Veneti". By 1468 he was firmly established in the Marche, near Ascoli Piceno, where he remained until his death in around 1493.

All of Carlo Crivelli's pictures are of religious subjects. His style was highly individual, with a strong element of late gothic fantasy. His masterly technique and extravagant attention to detail was also rather old-fashioned for its time. He left Venice too early to be influenced by Bellini's atmospheric art. He also still used raised plaster to give a three-dimensional effect to details such as drops of Christ's blood or the tears of mourners.

The best place to see his works in the Marche is in the *Duomo* and the *Pinacoteca Civica* in Ascoli Piceno, while you'll find other works in the *Pinacoteca Civica* in Ancona, the *Pinacoteca Civica* in Macerata, and in the small towns of Corridonia, Massa Fermana, Montefiore dell'Aso, Monte San Martino, Poggio di Bretta, Sant'Elpidio Mare, and Torre di Palme.

You may come across works by Vittore Crivelli; he was almost certainly Carlo's younger brother and they are known to have worked together on several occasions in the Marche. Little, however, is known about his life. Though a fine craftsman, his art never seemed to reach the masterly heights of his brother.

The Versatile Lorenzo Lotto

Lorenzo Lotto was born in Venice in around 1480 but spent much of his life elsewhere. He worked in Treviso and Bergamo, in northern Italy, as well as in the Marche. Towards the end of his life he settled in Loreto where he became a lay brother in the monastery of the Holy House in 1554. He died there two years later.

Lotto's paintings were strikingly original and often surprisingly inventive. In the words of the art historian Frederick Hartt: "he could ring a surprising number of changes [...] running from extreme naturalism, through attempts at the bizarre [...] to exultant lyricism of mood and colour".

You can see his works in the Marche at the Villa Colloredo-Mels in Recanati, the Pinacoteca Civica in Jesi, the Museo-Pinoteca in Loreto, the Pinacoteca Civica in Ancona, the Pinacoteca Civica in Cingoli, and in churches in Ancona, Mogliano and Monte San Giusto.

The Genius of Piero della Francesca

Long neglected, Piero della Francesca is now regarded as one of the greatest Italian Renaissance painters and his name is closely linked to the court at Urbino.

He was born sometime between 1410-1420 in Sansepolcro, just over the border in Tuscany. His earliest known painting is the *Madonna della Misericordia* in his native town but like many of his works it took years to complete – it was commissioned in 1445 for delivery within three years but was finally paid for some 17 years later.

A master of the impersonal, his mathematical clarity and absence of sentimentality produced images whose spiritual depth still confounds us. Always seeking to redraw the boundaries of art, he was also a great theorist and wrote two of the most important treatises of his time on perspective.

The last record we have of him painting was in 1478 but he lived on until 1492 – tragically blindness seems to have blighted his last years. Two of his finest works can be seen in Urbino – the *Flagellation of Christ* and the *Madonna of Senigallia*. His home town of Sansepolcro, just over the border in Tuscany, is worth visiting to see his fresco of the *Resurrection*, described by the British writer Aldous Huxley as "the greatest painting in the world".

The Divine Raphael

Raffaello Sanzio, better known in English as Raphael, was born in Urbino in 1483 – you can still visit the house where he was born.

Raphael's father, Giovanni Santi, was court painter to Duke Federico and a number of his paintings and frescoes can be seen in the *Palazzo Ducale* in Urbino, as well as in nearby towns. Of particular interest is the fresco of *Madonna and Child* in the church of San Domenico, Cagli, where the angel standing to the right of the throne is said to be a portrait of the young Raphael, then aged about eight.

After his father's death in 1494, Raphael studied with another Urbino painter, Timoteo Viti, before leaving the Marche to become a pupil under Perugino in Umbria. This marked the end of Raphael's connection with Urbino. His career and fame was built in Rome, where he lived until his untimely death in 1520 at the age of 37.

While there are few works by Raphael in the Marche, one of his finest pictures can be seen in Urbino's Ducal Palace – his famous portrait of a young woman, known as *La Muta* (The Silent One).

The best buildings

Roman remains

Ancona – Trajan's Arch by the port

Falerone – remains of a Roman theatre

Fano – the Arch of Augustus, gateway to the Flaminian Way

Furlo Gorge – hand-hewn tunnel built by Vespasian in AD 76 to take the *Via Flaminia*

Macerata – the amphitheatre at *Helvia Ricina*, just below the city

Urbisaglia – the remains of *Urbs Salvia*, including amphitheatre

Early Churches & Monasteries

Ancona – Cathedral of San Ciriaco, built on pre-Roman foundations

Fonte Avellana – a well preserved medieval monastery

Santa Maria A Pie' di Chienti – wonderful example of a "double-decker" romanesque church

Abbazia di Fiastra – one of Italy's great Cistercian abbeys

San Claudio al Chienti – double-decker 9th century church

Santa Maria di Portonovo – 11th century romanesque church built right on the Conero beach

Fortresses

Corinaldo – outstanding set of 14th century town walls

Mondavio – town walls and 15th century picture-postcard *Rocca*

Sassocorvaro – tortoise-shape 15th century castle sitting in the town's main square

Senigallia – The mighty 15th century seaside *Rocca Roveresca*

Tolentino – solid 14th century *Castello di Rancia*, just outside town

Medieval town architecture

Ascoli Piceno – its central square is one of the most elegant provincial squares in all Italy

Fabriano – a fine example of a provincial medieval town

Offida – fine gothic town hall

Renaissance architecture

Jesi – *Palazzo della Signoria*, a text-book example of the perfect Renaissance *palazzo*

Loreto – the Sanctuary of the Holy House

Urbino – Federico da Montefeltro's *Palazzo Ducale,* one of Italy's finest Renaissance palaces

Visso – Santuary of Macereto, a perfectly symetrical jewel of a church in the Sibillini mountains

Geography notes

The Marche form the eastern Adriatic seaboard of central Italy with the regions of Emilia-Romagna to the north and Abruzzo to the south. From the relatively narrow coastal plains the land rises sharply to the peaks of the Apennines which form a natural boundary with Umbria, Tuscany and Lazio to the west.

While the coastal areas are fairly heavily populated, the inland countryside is sparsely inhabited. The total population of the region is around 1.5 million with an average density of less than 150 inhabitants per square kilometre. The region covers just under 10,000 square kilometres.

The inland mountainous zones are mostly limestone and are noted for bare peaks, rushing torrents, dramatic gorges and many complexes of caves. In contrast, the areas nearer the coastal plain are celebrated for their fertile rounded hills crowned by ancient fortified towns.

The highest point in the Marche is Monte Vettore in the Sibillini Mountains at 2,476 metres. The huge rocky walls and crags in its eastern side, with such eerie names as Pizzo del Diavolo (Devil's Beard) and Gola dell'Infernaccio (Hell's Gorge), are every bit as dramatic as the landscape of the Dolomites. Monte Catria is the highest peak in the north of the region and reaches 1,700 metres.

The Marche has 180 kilometres of coastline and a number of long sandy beaches; apart from the limestone Conero peninsula, it is virtually all flat.

Economically, the region is mostly reliant on medium and small scale productive industries, often family-run. Shoes, clothing and furniture manufacture are amongst the most successful businesses. The relatively poor soil and the general movement away from the land has meant that agriculture now plays a lesser role, apart from the production of Verdicchio, the Marche's famous white wine in the central areas. By the coast, fishing remains an important activity.

Wherever you may find yourself in the Marche, the Apennine mountains are never far away. They form the region's western border and offer some of its finest scenery as well as providing a home for some of Italy's most fascinating wildlife. Large areas have now been designated natural parks.

The Parco Naturale dei Monti Sibillini, in the southwest, is the region's largest park, spreading over 40 km of mountain peaks and continuing westwards into Umbria. The most striking feature of the area is the large area of upland plain called the Piano Grande to the west, and mostly in neighbouring Umbria. In May and June, this sweeping expanse of treeless plateau, 1,250 metres above sea level, eight kilometres long and five wide, is transformed into a carpet of wild flowers.

Events

Almost everywhere you go, from the smallest villages to the largest towns, you'll find a crowded calendar of events, which frequently centres on the summer months. It includes two of the leading opera festivals in Italy and town festivals with fun and games, generally of the medieval kind.

Music and the arts

Rossini Opera Festival – Pesaro (annually, mid -August). www.rossinioperafestival.it

At Macerata, Open-Air Opera Festival in the Sferisterio arena (annually, late July to mid August). www.sferisterio.com

Other significant Marche cultural events include:

Ancona – The Teatro delle Muse has a strong opera, classical music and jazz season. www.teatrodellemuse.org

Ancona – Ancona Jazz Summer Festival, July. www.anconajazz.com

Castelfidardo – International Accordion Festival, late September. One of the world's leading events dedicated to the instrument. www.festivalcastelfidardo.it

Civitanova Marche – Civitanova Dance Festival, June-July. www.civitanovadanza.it

Falerone & Urbisaglia – TAU festival with classical theatre productions staged in two of the region's finest Roman amphitheatres – July & August. www.amatmarche.net

Fano – Carnevale, fun in February/March for carnival. www.carnevaledifano.com

Jesi – Opera season at the Teatro Pergolesi in autumn-winter. www.fondazionepergolesispontini.com

Polverigi – Festival Internazionale Inteatro, contemporary theatre at the villa comunale Nappi in June. www.inteatro.it

San Severino Marche – Blues festival in July. www.sanseverinoblues.com

Urbino – Musica Antica early music Festival in July. www.fima-online.org

These websites have events listings for the region, but are only in Italian:

- www.corriereproposte.it
- www.marcheinfesta.it
- www.eventiesagre.it
- www.laprimaweb.it

Eating and drinking

Most towns and villages have an eating event, or *sagra*, of some type which often takes place during late July or August and may coincide with medieval jousting or festivals. Generally the food is excellent, costs little and is accompanied by music and an atmosphere which is every bit as enjoyable as the food. Out of season, the food events tend to celebrate the harvest of a particular local speciality or the local wine. Here are a few of them:

April

Ascoli Piceno – Fritto misto all'italiana (festival dedicated to fried food)

June

Montecarotto – Verdicchio in festa (wine festival)

Pianello (near Cagli) – Sagra della Lumaca (snails)

July

Carpegna – Festa del Prosciutto

Castelplanio (near Jesi) – Sagra della crescia sul panaro (stuffed flat bread)

Corinaldo – polenta festival on third Sunday in July to commemorate the time when the town's people resisted a siege thanks to copious supplies of polenta.

Matelica – Sagra della Rana (frogs)

Porto San Giorgio – Festa del mare with a giant "frying pan"

August

Cingoli – Sagra di prosciutto e melone

Loro Piceno – Sagra del Vin Cotto (sweet "cooked" wine)

Massignano (near Ascoli Piceno) – Sagra delle frittelle (a fried sweet)

Monteprandone (near San Benedetto del Tronto) – Sagra delle olive fritte (fried stuffed olives)

Pedaso – Sagra Nazionale delle cozze (mussels)

San Severino Marche – Sagra del cece (chick peas)

Sassoferrato – Sagra del Cinghiale (wild boar)

Serra San Quirico (near Fabriano) – Sagra del coniglio in porchetta (roast rabbit with fennel)

Staffolo (near Cingoli) – Festa del Verdicchio (verdicchio wine festival)

September

Apiro (near Cingoli) – Sagra della polenta

Arcevia – Sagra dell'uva (grape festival)

Cupramontana – grape festival in the heart of Verdicchio wine country

Fano – Festival Internazionale del Brodetto (dedicated to Marche fish stew)

Fermo – Sagra della Polenta

Montecassiano – Sagra del pesce (fish)

Piandimeleto (near Urbino) – Festa del fungo (wild mushrooms)

Senigallia – Pane Nostrum (festival of bread)

October

Acqualagna (near Cagli) – Fiera nazionale del tartufo (truffle fair) – last weekend in October and first two weekends in November in the town that calls itself the "truffle capital".

Acquasanta Terme (near Ascoli Piceno) – Festa d'autunno (autumn produce)

Montemonaco (near Ascoli Piceno) – Sagra della Castagna (chestnut)

Sant'Angelo in Vado (near Urbino) – Mostra del tartufo bianco (white truffle)

November

Cartoceto – Festival of olive oil

Antique fairs

Street fairs selling antiques, bric-a-brac, the not-so-old stuff that is known in Italy as *modernariato*, and even what some might label "junk", have become popular across the peninsula and over 20 towns in the Marche now have a regular antiques market.

The main monthly fairs include Ancona on the last Sunday of the month and the Saturday before, Ascoli Piceno on the third Sunday and Saturday before, Fano on the second Saturday and Sunday, Pesaro on the third Sunday, Recanati on the first Sunday and Saturday before, and Tolentino on fourth Saturday and Sunday.

Fun and games

Every town of any size in the Marche now has its own *rievocazione storica*, a day or two of historically-inspired jollity usually featuring some form of knightly tournament between the different quarters of the town, a grand parade in sparkly renaissance costumes and, of course, plenty of enthusiastic eating and drinking to round off the event.

The grandest of them all is Ascoli Piceno's **Quintana** in August. The region's answer to Siena's celebrated Palio, it features a spectacular joust in the city's main square with horsemen tilting at a "quintain" as well as a procession of over a thousand people in historical costume.

Other outstanding examples of these summer events include **La Disfida del Bracciale** at Treia, an energetic ball game featuring a vicious wooden "bracelet" used to hit the ball, the **Contesa dello Stivale** at Filottrano featuring a race for a boot, and the **Caccia al Cinghiale** at Mondavio with archery, fireworks and a renaissance banquet. Other towns that feature notable *rievocazioni* include Acquaviva Picena, Cagli, Caldarola, Cingoli, Corinaldo, Corridonia, Fermo, Offagna, San Ginesio, Sant'Elpidio a Mare, Servigliano and Urbino.

The festivities carry on well into the night with open-air *taverne* – often a unique chance for the tourist to sample a quintessentially Italian festive atmosphere. A selection of the best of these are:

Disfida del Bracciale in **Treia** – a medieval ball game, on the first Sunday of August.

Quintana in **Ascoli Piceno** – jousting in Ascoli's main square on the first Sunday of August. The most authentic "medieval" goings on in the Marche.

Corsa alla Spada in **Camerino** – ancient games played out at the feast of the Town's patron, St Venanzio, on first Sunday after 17 May.

Contesa dello Stivale at **Filottrano** – first Sunday of August

Cingoli 1848 – 19th century fun and games through the streets of **Cingoli** in mid-August

Battaglia della Rancia – recreation of the 1815 battle between Murat and the Austrians at Tolentino, early May.

Festa del Duca in **Urbino** in honour of Duke Federico – the third Sunday in August.

Palio dell'Oca in **Cagli** – medieval games in the piazza to win a golden goose – mid-August.

Wild Boar Hunt in **Mondavio** – a medieval chase in the square – mid-August.

Palio della Rana in **Fermignano** – yes, a race with frogs in wheelbarrows – the first Sunday after Easter.

I Vlurd in **Offida** on Shrove Tuesday at the end of the carnival season flaming bundles – known as *i vlurd* – are taken in a procession round the streets.

Making a spectacle of religion

The Catholic church still plays a conspicuous public role in Italy despite falling numbers of regular churchgoers. And its sense of theatre can be witnessed in the numerous public religious spectacles across Italy. A number of towns across the Marche mark the week before Easter – particularly Good Friday – with full-scale costumed re-enactments of the biblical Passion of Christ. The most striking of these *passioni viventi* in the region include *La Turba* at Cantiano (PU), the *La Morte del Giusto* at Villa Musone, Loreto (AN), and the *Rievocazione storica della Passione di Cristo* at Mogliano (MC). Many other towns organize atmospheric processions on Good Friday featuring hooded *penitenti*, or penitents, walking barefoot through the streets, dragging a heavily decorated catafalque and accompanied by the town band playing funeral marches.

Still on a religious theme, the Sunday after the feast of *Corpus Domini*, or Corpus Christi, is frequently marked by an *infiorata* when the main streets of many towns in Italy are decorated with lavish quantities of flower petals in suitably religious designs. Towns in the Marche worth visiting to see good examples of these floral tapestries include Castelraimondo (MC), Fabriano (AN), Montefiore dell'Aso (AP), Ortezzano (FM), San Paolo di Jesi (AN) and Servigliano (FM).

Tours

Eight driving routes to explore the region

We have devised these eight tours to help you see the best if you're touring the region by car. They can all be easily driven in one day but many of the places on the way warrant more time. Bear in mind that though distances are short, many of the smaller inland roads are best driven at a leisurely pace, both to admire the views and negotiate the twists and turns.

Each tour is accompanied by a simple map to indicate the route but you'll want a detailed driving map of the region – we suggest the 1:200,000 maps of Umbria & Marche from either the Touring Club Italiano (TCI) or Michelin. Don't be afraid to make detours off the routes – making your own discoveries is half the point.

- Tour 1 **The lands of Montefeltro** – a jaunt through the northern reaches once ruled by the Dukes of Urbino.
- Tour 2 **In the footsteps of ancient Rome** – Roman remains on the *via Flaminia*, one of Europe's oldest roads.
- Tour 3 **From paper to stone** – Fabriano and Monte Catria with some glorious countryside.
- Tour 4 **The vineyards of Verdicchio** – a meander through the vineyards and hill-towns of the central Marche.
- Tour 5 **The heartland of the Marche** – a route packed with incident and some stately towns.
- Tour 6 **In the shadow of Monte Conero** – variety on a route from the sea to the hills.
- Tour 7 **The wild mountains of the Sibyl** – high roads in the southern upland stretches of the Marche.
- Tour 8 **Ascoli & Fermo's hidden heritage** – Ascoli Piceno is the star but smaller towns play some great cameo roles along the way.

Tour 1

The lands of Montefeltro

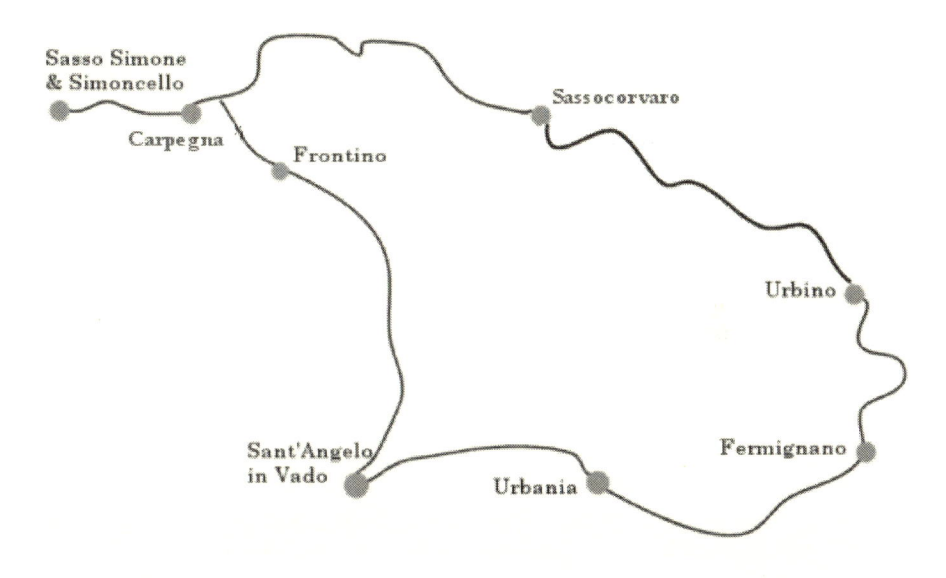

[Map showing locations: Sasso Simone & Simoncello, Carpegna, Frontino, Sassocorvaro, Urbino, Sant'Angelo in Vado, Urbania, Fermignano]

The uplands in the northern stretch of the Marche provide the backdrop to this tour of the lands once ruled over by the medieval lords of Montefeltro. Centred on the magical town of **Urbino**, one of Italy's most alluring Renaissance towns, the route takes in a scattering of delightful small towns set in ever-changing and breathtaking countryside.

On the way you can visit the impressive castle at **Sassocorvaro** right in the centre of town; you may recognise the hand of one of Renaissance Italy's greatest military architects, Francesco di Giorgio Martini. For it was he who either built or extensively remodelled many of the castles in the area in the 15th century during the rule of Federico da Montefeltro, the greatest of Urbino's dukes.

But the tour has other charms alongside the towns. Lovers of wild countryside will enjoy the high slopes of **Monte Carpegna** that contrast well with the softer hills on the earlier parts of the route. A traditional style of farming is still practised in much of the area and the landscape remains relatively unscathed by industry.

The pleasures of the table are also well represented along the way. Carpegna is famous for its ***prosciutto crudo***, or raw, cured ham - *coscia, sale, tempo e nient'altro* (thigh, salt, time and nothing else) as its publicity states. The ***pecorino*** ewe's milk cheeses are excellent in much of the area and in the northern reaches you will find the much prized ***formaggio di fossa***, a strong-flavoured cheese matured in sealed-up caves; try it with a dab of the excellent local honey. Truffles, or ***tartufi***, also feature on the menu in the area, although for the best fresh white and black truffles you'll need to visit in the winter. The beech woods of the area also produce a good crop of *funghi porcini*, the king of edible wild mushrooms.

The Route

Part I - Urbino to Carpegna

The journey starts from **Urbino** on its twin-peaked hill. (see page 119). Slow, twisting minor roads lead to the first stop at **Sassocorvaro**. Apart from a pretty setting beside an artificial lake, there is one overriding reason to visit this homely village - to see its splendid castle, which sits like a giant tortoise in the central square. Designed in 1475 by Francesco di Giorgio Martini for the powerful local Ubaldini family, it is reckoned one of his finest works.

The entrance gate leads into a fine Renaissance courtyard with a delicate balcony, around which are constructed the castle's three principal towers. Inside, the rooms are filled with a collection of pictures and bric-a-brac. The tiny 18th century private theatre with its elaborately frescoed ceiling is particularly noteworthy. The castle was used during the Second World War to hide many of Italy's finest works of art from Venice, Milan and Florence, as well as Piero della Francesca's Flagellation that you may have just seen in Urbino's *Palazzo Ducale*.

Winding along the valley of a rushing torrent the road now heads for **Macerata Feltria**. This small place has a modern part, noted for its spa establishment and the more interesting medieval core, **castello**, up above, around the old castle. The 14th century church of San Francesco with a pleasing gothic portal is worth looking out for while you stroll around.

From here our route takes you along roller-coaster roads with glorious views towards San Leo, in the neighbouring region of Emilia-Romagna. Pause for a while at **Pietrarubbia** to admire atmospheric rocky outcrops and the small hamlet, once abandoned and now restored with singular good taste and housing a smart art gallery.

Part II – Carpegna to Urbino

The twisting route now heads up the mountains to **Carpegna**, some 750 metres above sea level. The town takes its name from the eponymous cropped-topped mountain that dominates the countryside and offers great opportunities for trekking. The old centre has some fine buildings but the main attraction of the place is its setting. To the south west make a detour to see the dramatic rocky outcrops known as the **Sasso Simone** and **Simoncello**, both now standing in a regional nature park.

The tour now heads southwards through yet more idyllic countryside to the bustling town of **Sant'Angelo in Vado**. This small agricultural and commercial centre in mountain country has an attractive *centro storico* that warrants a stop (see page 112).

The tour now travels along gentler roads to the noble old town of **Urbania** with plenty of good reasons to stop (see page 118).

From Urbania head for **Fermignano**, a thriving small town just south of Urbino that warrants a brief stop to see the old centre with its picturesque ancient bridge and solid tower by the river Candigliano. It also has a long-established annual race with frogs in wheelbarrows on the first Sunday after Easter.

The countryside around is typical of the rolling hills backed by high mountains that surround Urbino. From here begins the winding climb back up to our starting point and a well-earned plate of soothing *passatelli*, Urbino's delicate pasta made from breadcrumbs, parmesan cheese and eggs and usually served in light broth.

Francesco di Giorgio Martini

No single architect had as great an impact upon the hill town landscape of the northern Marche as Francesco di Giorgio Martini (1439-1501). For a period of almost twenty years from 1476, under the dukedom of Federico da Montefeltro, he designed scores of fortresses and palaces around Urbino and as far south as Jesi each bearing the stamp which marked him out as an architectural visionary. He was also a talented painter and sculptor.

He was one of only a few artists from Siena to become known in other parts of Italy - he worked in the courts of Naples and Milan (where he was strongly influenced by Leonardo da Vinci) before arriving at Urbino in 1476. Federico da Montefeltro, a brilliant soldier and man of great culture, had been duke for only three years. His court had already become an important centre of culture and learning and now he wished to create a secure kingdom over which he could rule with his own brand of enlightenment. He quickly recognised Francesco di Giorgio's genius.

Places where his work can be seen include the fortresses of **Sassocorvaro** (perhaps the finest of them all), **Sant'Agata Feltria**, **San Leo**, **Fossombrone**, **Cagli**, and **Mondavio**, as well as work on the Ducal Palaces of **Urbino** (including the twin-turreted facade) and **Urbania**, the Palazzo della Signoria at **Jesi** and the church of San Bernardino in Urbino.

Tour 2

In the footsteps of ancient Rome

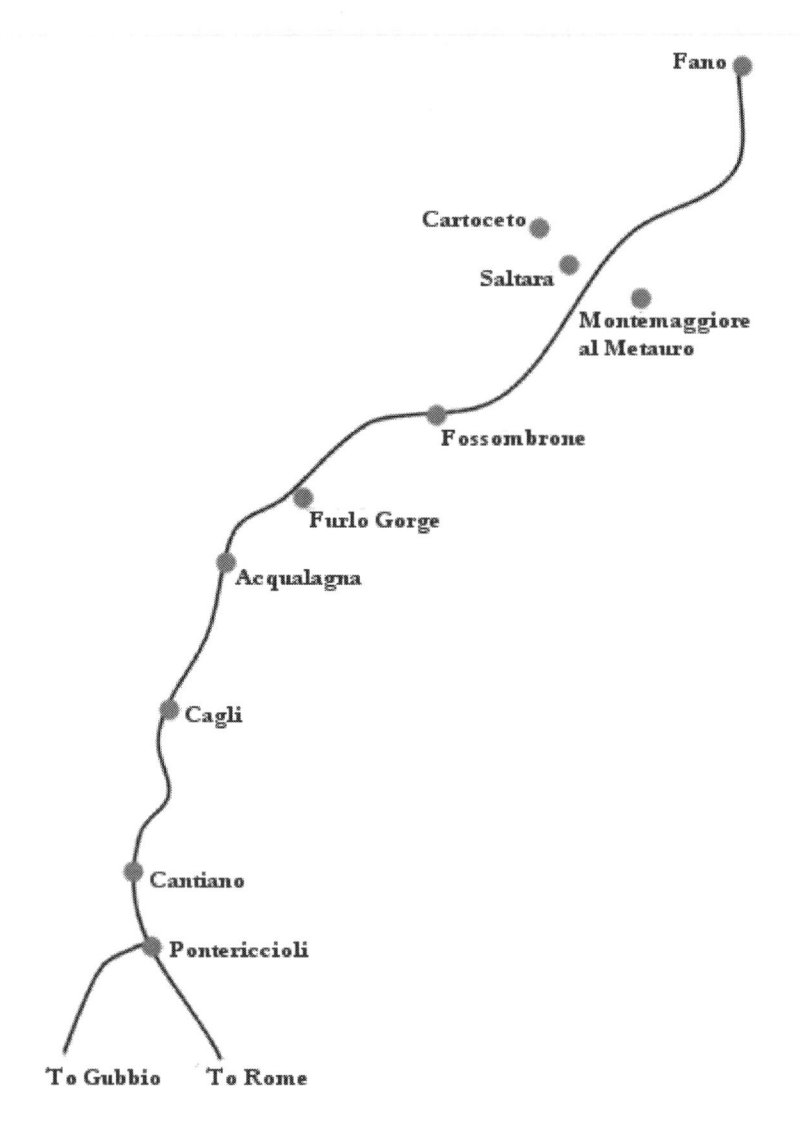

This route heads inland from the Adriatic coast along one of Europe's most historic roads and dips its toe into neighbouring Umbria. Ancient arches, bridges, walled garrison towns and even a Roman tunnel, still in use today, litter its path.

The *Via Flaminia*, or Flaminian Way, was built by the Roman Consul Gaius Flaminius in 220 BC and was one of Ancient Rome's most important highways, used by its great armies marching to the northern reaches of the Empire. Its importance continued into the Middle Ages when the Papal States valued it as a strategic highway and as a route for northern pilgrims heading to the shrine of St Francis at Assisi.

But interesting sights along the way are not limited to archaeological ruins. At **Fano**, the tour's starting point, you can paddle in the sea and window-shop in the smart streets of the beguiling old town. Between **Fossombrone** and **Cagli** you can admire the breathtaking **Furlo Gorge**, the scenic highspot on the route and now a regional nature park. This stretch runs parallel to a modern *superstrada* that has cleared the ancient road of all but local traffic. If time is short, however, you can use the modern dual-carriageway to hop between attractions. Shortly after the fine old town of **Cagli** the road reaches the Umbrian border. Here you can make a short detour to **Gubbio** in Umbria, one of Italy's best-preserved medieval towns.

Culinary delights on the route begin with the excellent fish at Fano - the *vongole*, or baby clams, are splendid in a dish of spaghetti. The small town of Acqualagna is noted for its truffles and up in the mountains the prized *porcini* mushrooms are abundant in the autumn.

The Route

Part I - Fano to the Furlo Gorge

The magnificent Roman arch built by the Emperor Augustus at **Fano** marks the point where the *Via Flaminia*, or Flaminian Way, reaches the Adriatic from Rome. Before setting out on the journey take time to explore this attractive old town and seaside resort (see page 91).

Now head inland across the fertile coastal plain either on the old road or on the modern *superstrada*. While light industry clutters the early part of the route, just off the road are a string of alluring small medieval towns up on the hills above the valley, worth visiting if you are in no hurry. These include **Montemaggiore al Metauro**, where Churchill watched the Allied assault on the Gothic Line during the Second World War, **Cartoceto**, noted for its local olive oil, and the medieval *borgo* of **Saltara**.

As the road begins to climb up towards the Apennine mountains, the first stopping place is **Fossombrone**. This small town, once the Roman *Forum Sempronii*, looks splendid from afar on the slopes of the Metauro valley. Although it has no single outstanding monument, it is a delightful collection of buildings and streets that bear witness to a prosperous past. The ruins that crown the town are of a castle built by the powerful Malatesta family. The town's centre boasts a pair of splendid arcaded streets lined with modest Renaissance palaces.

After Fossombrone comes the natural highspot of this section of the route, the heady limestone **Furlo Gorge** (page 95) Shortly after the gorge is the village of Furlo with several restaurants serving dishes dressed with local truffles. Also stop to admire the noble romanesque **Abbey of San Vincenzo** at the side of the old road.

Part II - The Furlo Gorge to Gubbio

The first town after the gorge is **Acqualagna**. Badly knocked about during the Second World War, it has little to detain the tourist for most of the year. However, during the last weekend in October and first two weekends in November it is transformed into Italy's "truffle capital" as it hosts the annual Truffle Fair - even before you arrive, the air is permeated with the smell of this exquisite underground *fungo*.

From Acqualagna the route heads for the medieval town of **Cagli**, which is well worth pausing to explore(see page 85).

The road now heads through the dramatic gorge of the Burano river towards Cantiano. Try to take the old Roman road rather than the parallel modern one, stopping to admire the large stones of the ancient Roman bridge on the way. **Cantiano** is a good example of an Apennine mountain town, with hard-faced medieval stone houses and an airy main square. It is also known for its horse breeding, and horse meat (*carne di cavallo*) often features on the menu. The old craft of charcoal burning is still practised in the beech woods that clothe the surrounding slopes.

Leaving Cantiano the modern road fades out, leaving you on the narrow twisting old road just before the junction for the *Contessa* road (SS452) which will take you on a 20-minute detour to the medieval gem of a town that is **Gubbio** in Umbria. Before turning off, stop to look at the Roman road-building remains at **Pontericcioli**.

Tour 3

From paper to stone - Fabriano, Monte Catria and its valleys

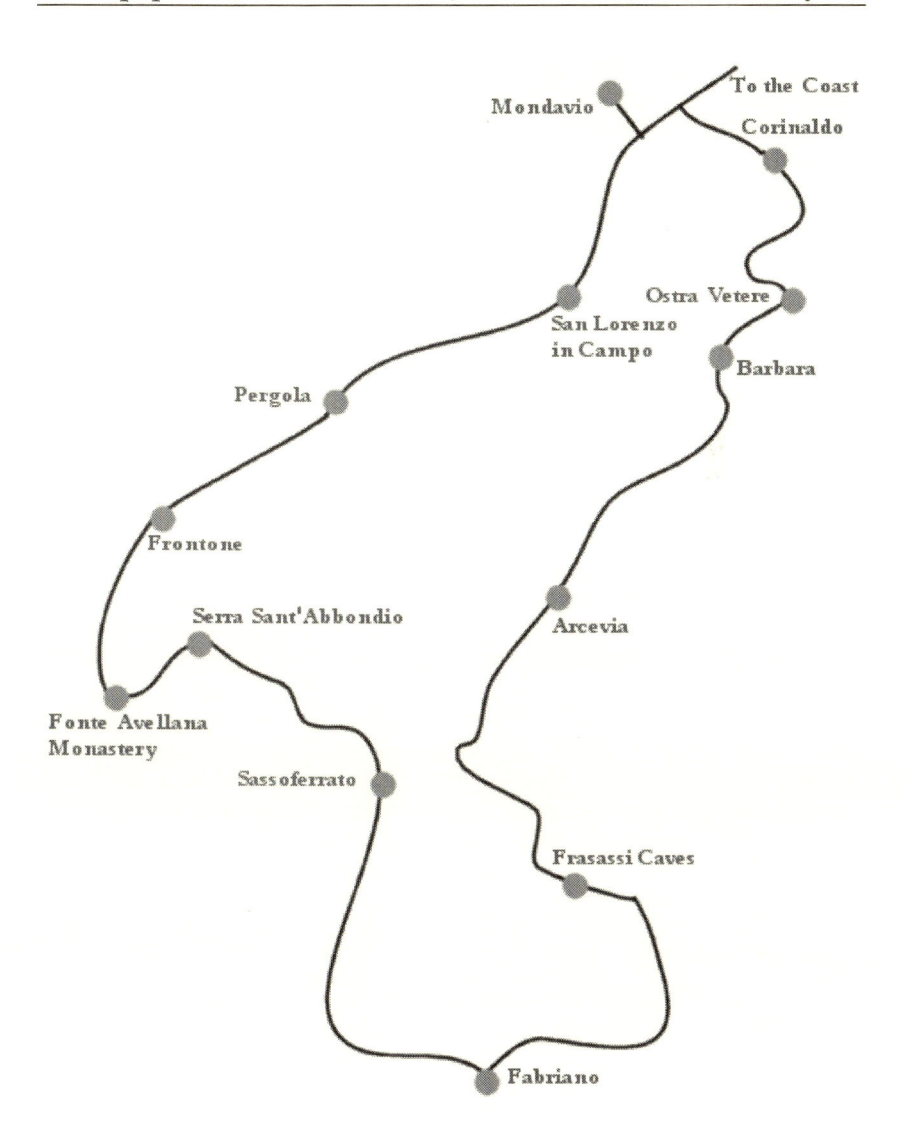

A chance to get away from the coastal plain and climb up into the mountains that divide the Marche from Umbria, this tour features spectacular landscapes, some of Europe's most dramatic caves, Italy's paper capital, and the atmospheric calm of an ancient isolated monastery.

The route starts at **Fabriano**, one of the world's oldest and most famous paper producing towns. No visit here would be complete without a trip round the paper museum, where you can still see paper being made by hand.

From here the road heads up towards the spurs of high **Monte Catria** and some of the most awesome scenery on the tour. Along the way we visit one of the region's oldest and most beautiful monasteries at **Fonte Avellana** and the mountain eyrie of **Frontone**.

The next stretch of the tour heads down through the gentler countryside of the Cesano valley, taking in two homely small towns - **Pergola** and **San Lorenzo in Campo** - before making a short detour to see the picture postcard walls and keep at **Mondavio**.

Another beguiling hill town awaits you at **Corinaldo** on the other side of the valley. Here you'll also find a shrine to its young 20th century saint, St Maria Goretti. The return stretch back to Fabriano winds through green open countryside and a string of peaceful small towns, including sprightly **Arcevia**, to arrive at the climax of the tour, the magnificent **Frasassi caves**.

Fabriano stands within easy reach of Ancona along the fast SS.78. There are several hotels to chose from in Fabriano as well as at Jesi, just south of this tour.

The Route

Part I - Fabriano to Fonte Avellana

Leaving Fabriano, take the signs which lead you along an attractive valley to the prosperous town of **Sassoferrato**. Follow the museum signs up to the solid citadel and medieval *borgo* high on a ridge above the modern town. Then stroll through the cobbled streets, past a fine gothic Franciscan church to arrive at the intimate Piazza Matteotti with its elegant arcades. The palace with the double ramp staircase, Palazzo dei Priori, houses the *Museo Archeologico Sentinate*, a collection of Roman mosaics, sculpture and funeral urns from the Roman city of *Sentinum* which stood on the plain just to the south of the modern town. It was here that the Roman army defeated the combined Samnite and Gallic forces in 295 BC. Recent archaeological excavations have unearthed various remains just to the south of the town but these are hard to find and strictly for the enthusiast. Nearby, in via Montanari, there is also a delightful museum of more recent relics from the rural past at the *Museo delle Arti e delle Tradizioni Popolari* as well as a museum of modern art.

The town was also the birthplace of the classical baroque painter Giovan Battista Salvi (1609–1685), better known as "Il Sassoferrato". His numerous devotional paintings, particularly of the *Madonna*, were highly popular in the Victorian age but went out of fashion in the 20th century; recently, however, in an age not so fearful of sentiment, they are having somewhat of a revival. You can see a couple of his works in the civic art collection in Palazzo Oliva.

The route now heads in the direction of Pergola, running alongside the single-track railway before turning left (just before a railway crossing) to Serra Sant'Abbondio and into the mountains. The pretty village of **Serra Sant'Abbondio** still has its walls to protect it. Through the medieval gateway, lines of crusty old houses line its narrow streets.

We now make a worthwhile detour to the **Monastery of Fonte Avellana** on the eastern flanks of Monte Catria in one of the most splendid settings imaginable. Its beauty is derived as much from the intentional poverty of the architecture as the magnificence of its proportions and the extraordinary size of the entire complex. Founded in 980, visited by Dante in 1310, and once presided over by St Peter Damian – one of the father figures of the Western monastic tradition - this is one of the few monasteries in the Marche to have retained a medieval form. Guided tours take you to the remarkable *scriptorium*. This was once an important centre for the production of illuminated manuscripts and was built with an ingenious system to maximise the hall's natural lighting. There is also the Dante Alighieri Library, with rows of rare *seicento* books and, of course, the church, with a simple single aisle and a flight of wide steps up to a raised presbytery. Beneath it, visit the crypt, supported by strong romanesque arches, and built with such finely-cut stone that it seems almost as if the walls have been carved straight out of the rock.

Dante praises the mountain and its monastery in Canto XXI of *Paradiso*:

> "Between two coasts of Italy, rise crags
> not far from where you live, so high
> that thunder sounds from far below their walls;
>
> they form a humpback ridge called Catria
> below which lies a holy hermitage
> that used to be a place of prayer alone."

Part II - Fonte Avellana to Mondavio

From the monastery the road snakes over a pass into the next valley, under the majestic peaks of mounts Catria (1,700 metres) and Acuto (1,527 metres), before descending to **Frontone**. Above the modern village stands a steep hill with just enough room on top for an imposing castle and medieval *borghetto*. As the last of a string of natural defences running from the sea to the impregnable Apennines, it has been fortified since the pre-Roman days when the area was garrisoned by the Eugubine tribes from Gubbio.

The well-restored *rocca* later helped to defend the southern border of the Duke of Montefeltro's lands and the triangular tower at the western end is said to be the work of Duke Federico's favourite architect, Francesco di Giorgio Martini. This windswept look-out (note the size of the rocks on the roofs to stop the tiles blowing away) gives a splendid prospect of the surrounding mountains.

Leaving the highlands behind us, we now drive into gentler countryside of wooded hills and valley farms. The traditional mixed farming system can still be seen here, with long rows of vines planted between narrow strips of grain.

Just off the road lies the elegant small town of **Pergola** whose quiet streets have a refined and distinctly 18th century air. The town's star attraction is the ***Bronzi Dorati***, lifesize Roman gilded bronze equestrian statues dating from the 1st century BC, found nearby in 1946. See page 106 for details.

Continuing on along the Cesano valley, we pass through the main street of **San Lorenzo in Campo** lined with dark-leaved evergreen oaks. On the left the tiny church of San Lorenzo dates back to the 7th century and is built on pillars from a pagan temple.

A short detour takes us up the northern flank of the valley to **Mondavio**. Bright geraniums and spreading cedars add a graceful tone to this beautifully preserved, small red-brick medieval hill town. The imposing fortifications that stand out from afar were built by Francesco di Giorgio Martini, one of Italy's most celebrated Renaissance military architects. They now house an entertaining 'living museum' (actually wax dummies) portraying life when the *Rocca* was built at the close of the 15th century for Giovanni della Rovere, son-in-law of Duke Federico da Montefeltro. There is also a grisly torture chamber to entertain the youngsters. If you're around in mid-August there is a jolly medieval boar hunt around the main square.

Part III - Mondavio to the Frasassi Caves

The next leg of the tour takes us across the Cesano valley to another fortified town, **Corinaldo**. It boasts almost a kilometre of some of the best-preserved 15th century defensive walls in central Italy - you can walk long stretches of the battlements while admiring the sweeping views. The town's other claim to fame is as the birthplace of the twelve-year-old modern martyr, St Maria Goretti. For further details on Corinaldo see page 89.

A few kilometres further on we arrive at **Ostra Vetere**, whose harmonious roof-line is topped by the exuberant dome of the town's neo-gothic church. Once inside the walls, note how the streets run in parallel terraces, joined to each other by steep flights of steps and the occasional tricky lane. Now take the road which travels along a wide open ridge to the village of **Barbara**, passing through the clock tower gateway at the bottom end of the village. The remains of the castle are more apparent as you leave through the *Castrum Barbarae* gateway at the top of the village - look back to see the tower and turrets.

Some 15 kilometres on we reach the noble town of **Arcevia**. Once you have twisted your way up to the top, the relative grandeur of the place comes as something of a surprise with several smart *palazzi* lining the main Corso Mazzini. Benign Piazza Garibaldi, half way along, is presided over by the town hall, topped by its 14th century tower. On the opposite side, a balcony under the arcades gives you a grandstand view out over the mountains to the south. The artistic high spot here is the church of **San Medardo**, half way up Corso Mazzini, where you can see two dramatically framed masterpieces by Luca Signorelli, painted while he was living here between 1507 and 1508, as well as an altarpiece by Giovanni della Robbia (1513).

Continuing on from here, the road curves through more dramatic scenery of wooded valleys towards Sassoferrato before turning off south to the soaring limestone cliffs of the **Frasassi Gorge**, the natural highspot of the tour. The **Frasassi Caves** are the largest caves in Italy and among the most spectacular in the whole of Europe (see page 94).

Before heading back to Fabriano, don't miss the opportunity to visit a hauntingly beautiful romanesque church by the little spa of San Vittore delle Chiuse (near the ticket office and car park for the caves). This small square *chiesetta* was built in the 11th century on chastely simple lines, and is a fine example of Byzantine-influenced architecture.

Further down the gorge towards the handsome, hill-top village of **Genga**, a steepish walk will take you to a remarkable octagonal neo-classical church built by the celebrated 18th century Roman architect Giuseppe Valadier high up on the rock face of the Frasassi Gorge. If you happen to be nearby over Christmas try to see the 'living crib' where 300 locals dress up to play the traditional roles in the Christmas story on 26 December and 3 January; it is claimed to be the largest such event "by extension" in the world.

Genga itself is notable as the native village of Annibale Della Genga, better known to history as Pope Leo XII (1760-1829).

Tour 4

The vineyards of Verdicchio

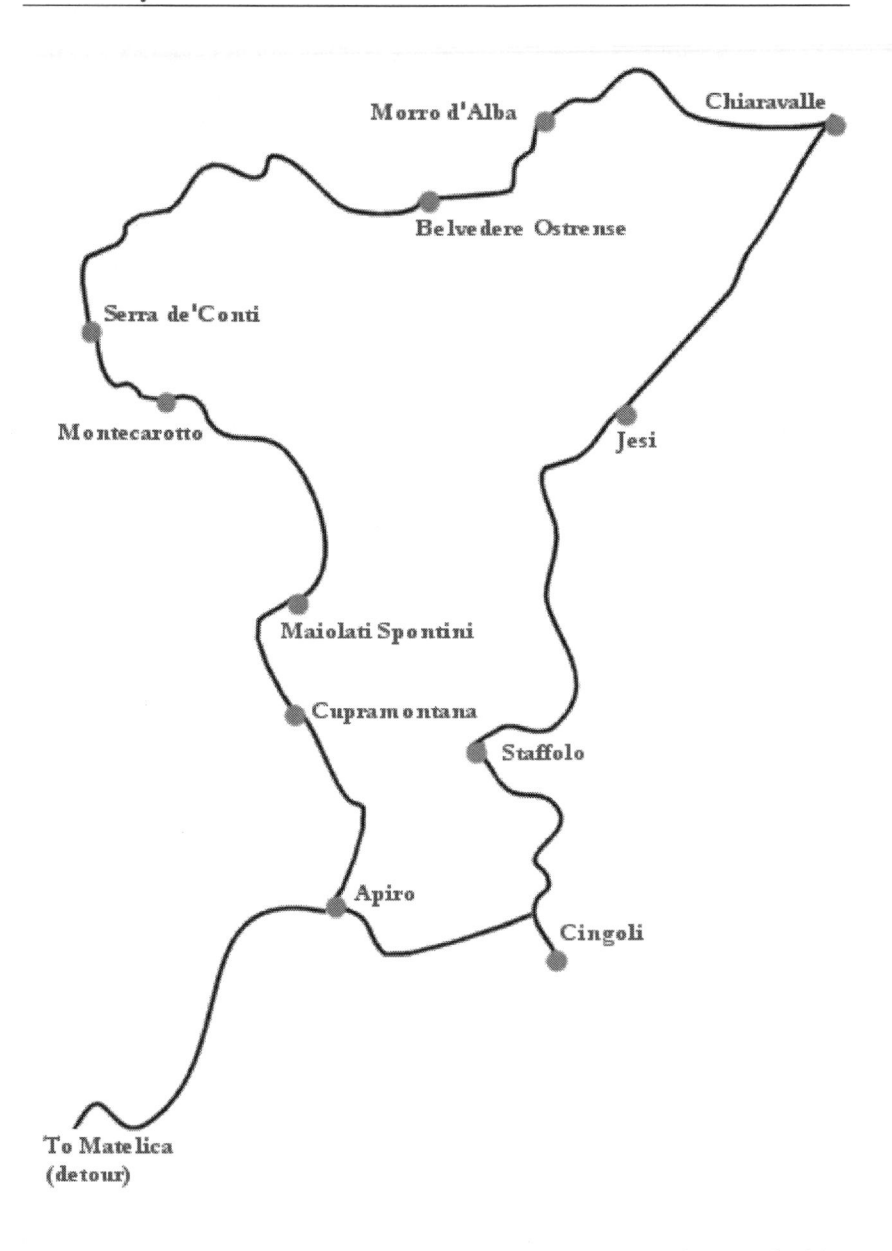

The foothills of the Apennines inland from Ancona produce Verdicchio, one of Italy's best known white wines. This tour meanders through vine-clothed valleys with the silhouettes of small medieval hill towns on every crest. The high peaks of the mountains in the distance provide an ever-present backdrop.

The route starts at the polished town of **Jesi** and visits **Cingoli**, another distinguished town. For the rest of the journey, the road passes smaller places, each with its own distinct character - **Ostra** with its narrow alleyways; **Apiro** with its crumbling stuccoed centre and handsome views; **Serra de' Conti** with its striking old quarter.

Racing pulses

Serra de' Conti is noted for its cultivation of *cicerchia* - now a little-known pulse that was once raised as an "insurance" against drought and famine when all other crops might fail, thanks to its ability to grow in extremely poor conditions.

The seeds of *Lathyrus sativus* are about the same size as peas but knobbly and buff coloured. Cicerchia has been recognised as one of the region's *prodotti agroalimentari tradizionali* and the humble legume now has an annual festival in its honour at Serra de' Conti.

They need to be soaked for at least 8 hours before cooking, changing the water 2 or 3 times, then boiled in plenty of unsalted water for around 40 minutes. Once cooked they should be left in the water and only drained when ready to be used - this avoids hardening as they cool. They are best used in hearty soups but also make a good substitute in most recipes for ordinary beans.

Along the way there are a number of *cantine*, or wineries, where you can try the green-tinged Verdicchio wines. And at **Morro d'Alba** there is a stop to taste the town's unique red wine, Lacrima di Morro d'Alba. For a rundown on Marche wines see page 19.

The main attraction along this route, however, is the landscape - homely rolling hills rising gradually towards the more stately peaks of the Apennines as we head south-west. For most of the way the tour follows winding backroads that follow the contours of the land with an uphill approach in low gear to each small town.

The Route

Part I - Jesi to Apiro

The spruce city of **Jesi** - sometimes known as the "Milan of the Marche" for its vibrant character - warrants at least a day to explore; you'll find full details on page 97. Follow the main road out of Jesi signposted *Roma* (all roads in central Italy really do seem to lead to Rome). Then turn off south for Cingoli.

The route now leaves the busy valley of the Esino as it climbs towards our first stop at **Staffolo**. The last stretch of the approach to this sturdy fortified medieval town boasts fine views - olive groves and vineyards spread out below the town walls. Large stretches of the intact walls now have houses built on top - a smaller version of the impressive walls of Jesi. During the second week of August the town gives itself over to the *Festa del Verdicchio*, a colourful festival dedicated to the local incarnation of Bacchus.

From here we now backtrack a short distance to the road for Cingoli and a splendid climb up to the "Balcony of the Marche" at **Cingoli**. This ancient hilltop town has plenty of treasures to explore (see page 88).

Again a short way back in our tracks to take the roller-coaster road for the hill top village of **Apiro**. This handsome looking place, some 500 metres above sea-level has a splendid backdrop of the solitary peak of Monte San Vicino, and an honest old centre with a fine tower and pretty church in its tight main square.

Part II - Apiro to Montecarotto

From Apiro the tour heads for the gentler hills around Cupramontana. Alternatively you might like to wind through country lanes and join the main SS256 to make a **detour** down south to the wine town of **Matelica**. Most of the life of this airy place revolves around the central Piazza Mattei, with its elegant 17th century fountain. Around it you'll find the town's chief attractions - the Loggia of the Ottoni family, built by the town's ruling family in 1511 and the 13th century Palazzo Pretorio, topped by an 18th century tower. In one of the side-chapels of the church of the Suffragio, search out Salvator Rosa's tortured painting of the Crucifixion and souls in Purgatory. Also worthy of note are the cathedral, with its 15th century bell tower, in Corso Vittorio Emanuele, and the church of the Maddalena, with its romanesque portal and facade. Before you leave, be sure to buy a couple of bottles of the town's own Verdicchio, *Verdicchio di Matelica,* some of the best you'll taste.

Back on course, our route makes for the agricultural market town of **Cupramontana**. Standing in a typical gently-rolling Marche landscape amidst Verdicchio vineyards, this is one of the most important centres for wine production and a good place to stock up with a few more bottles.

Heading back down to the more developed Esino valley, make a brief stop at **Maiolati Spontini**. In this small village the opera composer Gaspare Spontini (1774-1851) was born. He is buried in the church of San Giovanni, under an august neo-classical monument carved by Canova. The small Spontini museum, opposite the church in the house where he died, contains a collection of his manuscripts and possessions. The village also has fine balcony views over the valley below.

The tour now dips down to the valley, briefly joins the main road then quickly turns off to return to more beguiling countryside as we head for **Montecarotto**. For a change, the heart of this compact little *borgo* is at the bottom of the hill in Piazza della Vittoria. Here two fairytale towers, all that is left of a medieval castle, greet you as you drive in.

Part III - Montecarotto to Jesi

Following a particularly memorable stretch of country road, the tour winds down the creases of a valley with fine views as we head for **Serra de' Conti**. The first sight of its old centre is striking - high walls with elegant lofty *palazzi* and a strong architectural unity. Pause awhile to wander the hidden corners of this elegant small place. Its heart lies in Piazza Leopardi with a fine octagonal tower.

From Serra de' Conti the route follows tight curves to join the main SS360 road in the Misa valley. Follow the signs for Senigallia and speed towards the turning for **Ostra**. This imposing walled town is strung out along a ridge overlooking the valley. Its old centre, topped by the noble *Torre Civica* and Piazza dei Martiri, its red-brick main square, has plenty of attractive details to amuse the eye. Look out for the prosperous looking 18th century *palazzi* along the main Corso Mazzini.

Splendid views again accompany you as the tour heads south for a brief pause at **Belvedere Ostrense**, a sober small town with sturdy walls and airy panoramas.

Then on to **Morro D'Alba** with occasional glimpses of the Adriatic Sea only 10 kms away.

The pleasing old part of this rocky village is embraced by an escarpment wall dating back to the second half of the 15th century. Atop these walls runs a remarkable walkway pierced by porticoes that offers ever-changing views of the delightful countryside around. There is another excellent reason to stop here - to try its celebrated red wine, Lacrima di Morro d'Alba. A heady garnet wine made from the local *Lacrima* grape with a distinctive hint of berries and an elegant finish.

From Morro d'Alba you can either head straight back to Jesi or take a slightly longer route via **Chiaravalle**. This busy town has one good reason for you to stop – to see the Abbey of Santa Maria in Castagnola, often known simply as the Abbey of Chiaravalle. Founded in 1126, it is one of only a few monasteries founded in Italy by the Cistercian monks of Clairvaux from France. An outstanding and rare example of ecclesiastical gothic architecture in the region, it has a striking facade. The town was also the birthplace in 1870 of Maria Montessori, the founder of the Montessori method for educating children.

Tour 5

The heartland of the Marche

Many of the Marche's medieval hill towns were already thriving centres by the 15th century and most were left little altered when the Renaissance winds of change swept through the rest of Italy. As a result, this area boasts some of the finest early architecture in the whole of central Italy, such as the churches of **San Claudio al Chienti** and **Santa Maria a Piè di Chienti** which stand within a few kilometres of each other, as well as scores of perfect small medieval town centres.

This tour explores some of these places, taking in **Sant'Elpidio a Mare** and the tiny walled town of **Monte San Giusto**, before heading down past **Fiastra Abbey** and on to **San Ginesio** with its handsome town square.

From here, we head back northwards to visit the miniature university town of **Camerino**, picture-book **San Severino Marche,** and the tomb of Saint Nicholas of **Tolentino**. We also stumble across relics of earlier settlements, including Roman amphitheatres at **Urbisaglia** and **Villa Potenza.** The trip starts and ends at **Macerata,** the capital of one of the Marche's five provinces that stands just half an hour away from Ancona.

The Route

Part I - Macerata to San Ginesio

Macerata, world famous for its open-air opera festival, has several good hotels and makes an ideal base for this tour (see page 100). Heading south from Macerata, follow the signs to Civitanova Marche. The route drops down into the broad valley of the Chienti river, then heads eastwards along the SS.485. Our first visit is to the romanesque church of **San Claudio al Chienti** (just north of the main road) to see one of the Region's earliest and most curious churches. Its shape, quite unlike any other church in the Marche, is the first thing to strike you

- it is in fact two churches, built one above the other, with separate entrances and flanked by two cylindrical towers. Created between the 5th and 7th centuries, probably on the ruins of a villa which formed part of the Roman city of *Pausulae*, it was built using material from the ancient ruins. Its present shape dates from the 11th and 12th centuries. Inside, both the upper and lower churches are square in form, and supported on four solid central pillars.

A few kilometres further east along the SS.485 lies another magnificent early church, **Santa Maria a Piè di Chienti**. This beautifully preserved romanesque construction was built in the 9th century. Once again double-decker in form, this time the upper floor is built within the church at the further end of the high central nave. The 14th century frescoes in the apse above the upper altar are all the more powerful in their striking contrast with the remainder of the simple brick interior.

Leaving the modern ribbon development along the floor of the Chienti valley, we now head southwards to **Sant'Elpidio a Mare**. Despite its name, this worthy medieval town is not by the sea, but overlooks it from the safety of a hilltop stronghold. Through the Porta Marina and into the central Piazza Matteotti is the enigmatic Torre dei Cavalieri Gerosolimitani, built by the Knights of Malta in the 14th century, together with two churches and the Town Hall - inside, the municipal art gallery has a magnificent 18-panel painting by Vittore Crivelli.

Passing **Montegranaro** (shoe factories now surround this hill town, though the *centro storico* still boasts some medieval architectural relics) we reach **Monte San Giusto**. The narrow streets of this town, like many others, were never designed for the motor car and you are well advised to park outside the town walls. Search out the Church of Santa Maria in Telusiano, a few metres from the pretty central piazza to see one of Lorenzo Lotto's great masterpieces, a *Crucifixion*, painted in 1531 when the Venetian master was at the height of his career.

A few kilometres away in **Corridonia**, the parish art collection, next to the Church of S. Pietro e Paolo (half way up via Cavour), houses another masterpiece, Carlo Crivelli's *Madonna with Suckling Child*. You won't fail, however, to miss the town's most conspicuous sight. The vast monument to Filippo Corridoni at the top of the town was built in the 1930s to honour a local First World War hero; the town, previously known as Pausola, was renamed Corridonia at the same time. The white Roman travertine stone, so beloved of fascist architects, hardly blends with the warm brick of the surrounding buildings but the monument undoubtedly stands as an interesting example of the fascist architecture of the period. Passing on through **Petriolo** (note the unusual stubby cylindrical gateway which the road passes through on its way out of the town) we drive into the gentler scenery of the Fiastra valley.

The noble old **Fiastra Abbey**, (open May-June weekends only; July- Sept daily) is one of the great Cistercian abbeys to be founded under the wing of Clairvaux in France. Apart from its splendid setting, it has delightful frescoes by the Salimbeni brothers and a fine Renaissance cloister. Part of the building now houses an archaeological museum with finds from the nearby Roman ruins of *Urbs Salvia*, and a collection of antique rural artefacts. The whole area is a *Riserva Naturale*, an idyllic spot for country rambles, carefully protected by the World Wildlife Fund.

A few kilometres further south near **Urbisaglia**, stand the remains of *Urbs Salvia*, an archaeological site with things you can actually see - the amphitheatre is one of the region's most conspicuous Roman ruins.

> **Urbs Salvia**
>
> The remains of the Roman town of *Urbs Salvia*, founded around the 1st century BC, lie a short distance away from modern day Urbisaglia, 15 kilometres south-west of Macerata. The site is now preserved as an archaeological area.
>
> The amphitheatre, built in AD 75-76, has survived remarkably intact and is still used for summer performances of classical drama. It is oval in form, with a diameter of around 90 metres along the main axis and 70 metres along its narrower axis and stands on an area of flat ground, about 200 metres outside the town's eastern gate. It was originally entirely surrounded by a portico and had two entrances to the arena at opposite ends of the main axis, while spectators reached the auditorium through 12 *vomitoria*, or underground passageways.
>
> A frescoed *cryptoporticus*, or enclosed gallery, surrounded what was once probably a nearby temple to the goddess Salus Augusta.
>
> The large cistern on the northern edge of the town, comprising two long identical chambers with an overall storage capacity of around 100 cubic metres, was once fed by an underground aqueduct carrying water from the nearby mountains.
>
> In addition to the amphitheatre, there is also a theatre, 104 metres wide, built before AD 23 on the hillside below the medieval town of Urbisaglia. The remains of both its stage and semi-circular auditorium are clearly visible.
>
> By the 1st century AD Urbs Salvia had become a powerful town, but was destroyed by the Visigoths under the leadership of Alaric in AD 409-410.

Some 8 kilometres on from Urbisaglia take a short detour to **Loro Piceno**, a delightfully intact old town topped by a 13th century castle. The town is renowned as the centre for the production of *vino cotto* (see page 20).

Back on the route, drive up to **San Ginesio,** a striking town with a strong medieval stamp and breathtaking views of the mountains. The beautiful central piazza is named after the town's most famous son, Alberico Gentili (1552-1608), Regius Professor of Civil Law at Oxford University and one of the most important figures in the development of the modern principles of public international law. He was forced to flee Italy in 1579 because of his protestant leanings. His statue is overlooked by the splendid Collegiate Church - its romanesque portal is topped by an unusual gothic brick facade while the tower to one side has a distinctive onion dome. Inside, visit the crypt which is decorated with delightful early frescoes by Lorenzo Salimbeni (1406).

Part II - San Ginesio to Camerino

Heading back northwards, we trace our way along country lanes, following the signs for Caldarola. As with so many other Italian towns, **Caldarola** is inextricably linked with the fortunes of one dynastic family. The Pallotta family produced four cardinals and reached its heyday in the last decade of the 16th century when Cardinal Evangelista Pallotta transformed the family castle into his summer residence. For more details of this appealing town see page 86.

Our journey now takes us down to the busy main SS.77 road and on towards Camerino but no wine enthusiast should lose the opportunity of making a 15 km detour to taste the sparkling red wine of **Serrapetrona**, which stands on the opposite side of the Chienti Valley. *Vernaccia di Serrapetrona* is normally a sweet dessert wine but is also produced in a somewhat drier *secco* version which goes particularly well with the local soft *ciauscolo* salame.

Back on the SS.77, we travel westwards as far as the proud ruins of the Rocca di Varano which stand guard over this stretch of the valley pass, before turning north to arrive at the noble university town of **Camerino**. For details of this attractive town see page 87.

Part III - Camerino to Tolentino

Leaving Camerino, now head north past **Castelraimondo** before turning eastwards. If you have time, visit the village of **Gagliole**, just north of the main road, with its well preserved 14th century walls and castle.

The tour now arrives at **San Severino Marche**. Founded around AD 550 after the Goths had destroyed the Roman settlement of *Septempeda* further down the hill, this homely town has a happy mix of medieval and Renaissance buildings. Its outstanding feature is an unusual elliptical main square, Piazza del Popolo, flanked by shady arcades. Search out the *Pinacoteca*, or art gallery, in Via Salimbeni 39, to see Pinturicchio's sumptuous *Madonna della Pace* and some endearing pictures by the brothers Lorenzo and Jacopo Salimbeni. You can see more of their work in the nearby romanesque church of San Lorenzo in Doliolo.

A dish for a general?

The central and southern tracts of the Marche is the best area to try one of the region's most celebrated pasta dishes – *Vincisgrassi*. This refined *primo* is a local variation of baked *lasagne* with a *ragù*, or meat sauce, that traditionally includes chicken giblets and sweetbreads or bone marrow. Some cooks maintain that the sheets of pasta should be made with a little added *vino cotto* or marsala.

Many will tell you that the dish was named by a cook from Macerata in honour of Alfred von Windisch-Graetz, an Austrian general fighting against Napoleon in 1799 during the siege of Ancona. However, a *marchigiano* cookery book of 1781 features a similar recipe for a type of lasagna called *Princisgras*, said to be so named as it was rich enough to be fit for a prince.

We now return to the Chienti valley to visit the bustling market town of **Tolentino** and the basilica dedicated to its own saint, St Nicholas of Tolentino, and decorated with the Marche's most outstanding medieval frescoes (see page 117).

Part IV - Tolentino to Macerata

Just east of Tolentino, the swallowtail battlements of the **Castello della Rancia** come into view just off the main road. This solid square castle was built as a Benedictine abbey in the 12th century and transformed into a castle in 1357 by the ruling Da Varano family. It has been the scene of a number of battles, the last of which was the defeat of Joachim Murat, the King of Naples and Napoleon's brother-in-law, whose first 19th century bid to unify Italy was thwarted by Austrian troops in May 1815 - the battle is re-enacted each May in a colourful event with hundreds of extras. The castle has been restored and opened to the public.

Leaving the Chienti valley once again, we turn northwards to the small town of **Pollenza**. Within its brick ramparts, the single main street, via Roma, strings together three intimate *piazze*. The town is noted for antique furniture restoration and, as well as a number of workshops outside the walls, there are a handful of shops here to browse around. At the far end of the town, the sumptuous Church of San Biagio, decked out in perfect neo-classical style, seems almost too grand for a place as unassuming as this. The town's only other claim to (modest) fame is the Marche's only bust to the composer Verdi, which stands outside the theatre in Piazza della Libertà

Heading further north, the road crosses the valley of the River Musone to **Treia**, standing high on a long narrow hilltop. This papal stronghold was besieged during the wars against the Ghibellines. But nowadays its atmosphere is altogether more benign and the fortifications along its solid ramparts have been replaced with houses and balconies decked with washing. Torre Onglavina (or Torre di S. Marco) which stands imposingly on a rocky spur, is all that remains of the castle. On a clear day it offers a sweeping panorama of the Marche region, from the Apennine mountains to the west as far as Monte Conero and the Adriatic Sea to the east. The town has become famous for the annual *Disfida del Bracciale*, played out in the first Sunday of August.

This fast and demanding ball game dating from Renaissance times is played with three players in each team. Each player wears a fearsome-looking cylindrical wooden *bracciale,* or bracelet, over his hand. This has a flat top and wooden teeth around the side. By hitting the ball against a wall with the *bracciale,* each team scores points against the other until the game is won.

Returning to Macerata, pause just before **Villa Potenza** at the ancient remains of *Helvia Ricina*. When the Visigoths destroyed this Roman settlement in the 5th-6th century, its inhabitants took refuge on higher ground and founded the city of Macerata. Remains of the old city can still be seen, including the large amphitheatre, which stands just by the junction with the SS571, as well as a stretch of stone-paved roadway.

Tour 6

Under the shadow of Monte Conero

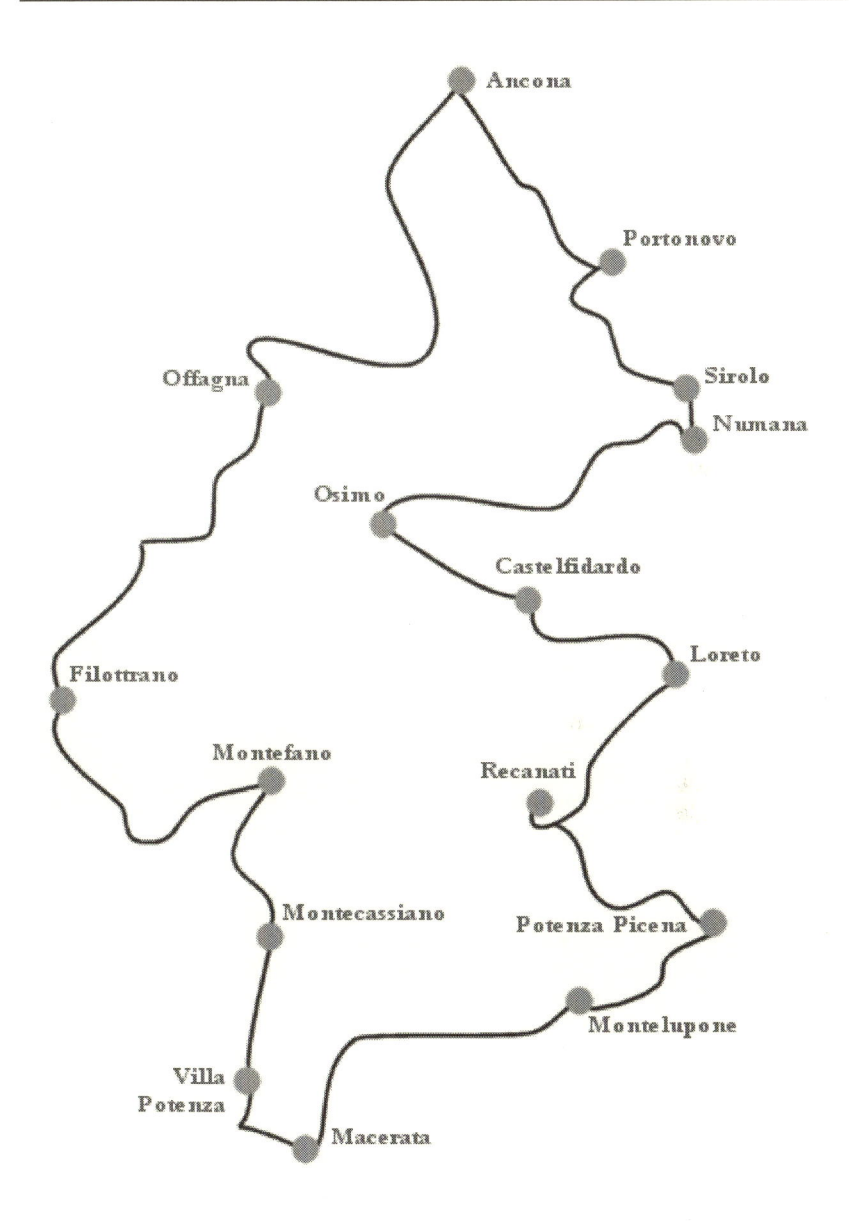

[Map showing tour route with the following locations: Ancona, Portonovo, Sirolo, Numana, Offagna, Osimo, Castelfidardo, Loreto, Filottrano, Montefano, Recanati, Potenza Picena, Montecassiano, Montelupone, Villa Potenza, Macerata]

    The route explores some of the towns and countryside lying within easy reach of **Ancona,** the capital of the Marche. This bustling city is the main gateway to the area both by plane and ferry, giving the place the atmosphere of a Mediterranean frontier. The influence of the East is also evident in some of its earliest architectural attractions - don't miss the Cathedral of San Ciriaco, on the

63

hill above the port - parts of the Byzantine mosaic floor of the original 6th century church can still be seen.

Our route avoids the busy city arteries and leaves by the backdoor along quieter and prettier roads to explore the seaside scenery of **Monte Conero**, some of the finest coastline in the whole of the Marche. It then heads for a short distance inland to visit five splendid hill towns, each with its own particular fascination. From the tomb of St Joseph of Copertino in **Osimo,** we travel to **Castelfidardo,** the capital of the accordion, and on to the Marche's most important place of pilgrimage, the Sanctuary of the Holy House at **Loreto** before arriving at the patrician town of **Recanati**, home of Italy's great Romantic poet, Giacomo Leopardi, as well as the operatic tenor, Beniamino Gigli.

The next leg of the tour takes us to one of the finest surviving 18th century gardens in Italy before heading across to the provincial capital of **Macerata**. The attraction of the final stage of the tour is the scenery, with some extra bonuses, including a Roman amphitheatre and a string of beautiful small hill towns which still remain well off the tourist track.

The Route

Part I - Ancona to Loreto

From the port, we head eastwards through the city to the coast road, and pick up the signs for Monte Conero. The road soon begins to rise and within a short while leaves the city suburbs to arrive at the slopes of **Monte Conero**. After a few more kilometres the mountain's solitary limestone peak comes into view. At 572 metres, this is the highest point along this stretch of the Adriatic coast and offers some spectacular views. For details of the Conero riviera see page 102.

A short detour takes you down to the beach resort of **Portonovo** and the early romanesque church of Santa Maria. Built between 1034 and 1048, its curious form is unique in Italy and looks as if it might be more at home in Normandy.

Back on the main road, after eight kilometres, another left turn takes you on a second detour up to the highest point on the mountain reachable by car, and worth the trip just for the views. Here you'll find the **Badia di San Pietro**, built in the 12th century as a Benedictine Hermitage and now a grand hotel. The area is also a regional nature park and a web of signed footpaths cover the peak. On the summit, traces of a Palaeolithic settlement dating back 100,000 years have been discovered - the earliest signs of human presence in the region.

Returning to the main road, we now head down to the southern flanks of Conero to visit **Sirolo**. Its balcony piazza, flanked on two sides by a spruce medieval centre, teeters high above the sea, offering magnificent views. Its sister resort, **Numana**, lies further down the slope, at beach level. The port dates back as far as the 8th century BC - various bronzes and pieces of pottery found in the area can be seen in the *Antiquarium* in via La Fenice, in the centre of the old town. You'll find more on these resorts on page 102.

Leaving the coast behind we now travel inland to visit four important hill towns which lie only a few kilometres away - follow the signs for Osimo. Driving along the plain below the slopes of Monte Conero, the road passes vineyards producing Rosso Conero, one of the Marche's DOC wines - and its finest red. There are several *cantine*, or wineries, in the area where you can stop to buy a bottle or two, or simply to taste this rich, full-bodied wine.

Our next destination is the homely town of **Osimo** which looms ahead of you on the crest of a hill. Enjoy the views out over classic Marche countryside as the road rises up towards the town (see page 105).

Our next town on the route is **Castelfidardo**, about five kilometres away. The land below this statuesque small hill town was the scene of a celebrated battle in the fight for the Unification of Italy, when the Piedmont army routed the "crusaders" of the Papal forces in 1860. It now styles itself the world capital of the accordion, or *fisarmonica*. In its *Museo Internazionale della Fisarmonica* you can see more than 150 examples of the instrument. The town still has a thriving musical instrument industry and claims that the piano accordion was developed here in 1863 from the more primitive Austrian squeeze box. If you are here in late September, come to the International Accordion Festival and discover that there are musicians who can transform the sound of this humble instrument with exceptional artistry.

The high, gleaming dome on the next hillside suggests that our next stop is no ordinary town. **Loreto** stands second only to Assisi and Rome as a place of Roman catholic pilgrimage. For further details on the town see page 99.

Part II - Loreto to Macerata

A few kilometres on from Loreto, we reach **Recanati**. The quiet nobility of this attractive place warrants a relaxing pause on the journey. This was the birthplace of Giacomo Leopardi, one of Italy's greatest Romantic poets and here you can stroll up to Piazza Leopardi, the town's urbane central piazza, and spot the plaques quoting the poet's lines on the buildings and monuments of his home town. For full details see page 110.

Our journey now takes us further southwards, crossing the valley of the River Potenza and the busy SS.571 and up to **Potenza Picena**, sitting within its sturdy walls. From the shade of the public gardens, you can enjoy fine views back over Loreto and Recanati with Monte Conero visible behind.

A ten-kilometre detour takes us to **Giardino Buonaccorsi**, which the celebrated garden writer Georgina Masson describes as "one of the most fascinating and least known of all gardens in Italy". It is the perfect example of an 18th century Italian garden and all the more amazing as the clock seems to have stopped, leaving it exactly as it must have been two hundred or so years ago.

Back at Potenza Picena, the road ripples along the ridge to the small medieval town of **Montelupone**. The road pierces the well-preserved walls, complete with their observation towers, through Porta del Cassero (*cassero* means castle keep, the remains of which can be seen in the public garden just to the left). The central Piazza del Comune is overshadowed by the tall tower of the *Palazzo del Podestà* with its striking battlements. Continuing along the ridge, the road passes through

Madonna del Monte before arriving at the city of **Macerata**. You'll find all the details on this distinguished town on page 100.

Part III - Macerata to Offagna

Head down from Macerata to the valley of the river Potenza, following the signs for Ancona. Crossing the river at **Villa Potenza**, you'll come across a large amphitheatre on the left of the main road. These are the remains of the ancient settlement of *Helvia Ricina*. When the Visigoths destroyed it in the 5th-6th century, its inhabitants ran away to higher ground and founded Macerata. Excavations have also uncovered an ancient embankment along the riverside and a stretch of ancient stone-paved roadway nearby.

Continuing northwards, we leave the main road to make for **Montecassiano**. Its small *piazza* is particularly worth a visit. The solid 15th century *Palazzo Comunale*, built over a shady portico, has three beautiful bottle-glazed windows. Steps lead through an archway to one side, up to the parish church, topped by a stubby spire. Inside the sober gothic brick interior, there is a refreshingly unrestored terracotta altarpiece by Mattia Della Robbia (1527), a lesser-known member of the famous Florentine artistic family.

Driving on to the pretty town of **Montefano**, the attraction here is the **Castello di Montefiore,** just outside. Built in the 14th century, it was later so well adapted to artillery defence that it remained intact through the centuries and it was the only the bombs of the Second World War that succeeded in damaging it. Since then, however, it has been sensitively restored and has a dramatic gateway and ramp which take you up to the castle keep.

Driving back through Montefano, our route now takes us in the direction of Jesi, passing through **Filottrano** with its church of San Francesco - a good example of late baroque architecture - before turning eastwards through delightful open countryside, back in the direction of Ancona.

The final stop is at **Offagna**, dominated by the solid tower of its picturesque 15th century *rocca*, or castle. Just below it, the *Palazzo Municipale* , adorned with noble coats of arms, adds to the attractions of this attractive small town. Heading back on the home stretch of the journey, we are once again among the vineyards that produce Rosso Conero.

Rosso Conero

This full-bodied ruby wine is the best known and noblest of the region's *vini rossi*. It has had a DOC label since 1967, and from 2006 it has had the coveted DOCG classification for its *riserva* version. It is grown in a comparatively small area, bounded by Offagna, Osima, Castelfidardo, Numana and Sirolo. The wine must be made from at least eighty-five per cent Montepulciano grapes, with up to fifteen per cent Sangiovese. See page 19 for more on the region's wines.

Tour 7

The wild mountains of the Sibyl

The **Sibillini mountains** offer some of the most breathtaking scenery in the whole of central Italy. The area, however, still remains off the usual tourist beat. The roads along this route remain almost deserted apart from winter skiers and intrepid ramblers in high summer. Yet, though they twist about through some of the Marche's remotest areas, they are generally reasonably easy to drive.

The mountains take their name from a legend that one of the sibyls - the prophetesses of classical mythology - hid here in a cave on Monte Sibilla known as the *Grotta della Sibilla* when she was chased out of the Underworld.

The literal highspot of this tour is a visit to the solemn upland plateau of **Piano Grande**, one of Italy's natural wonders, guarded by the solitary hill village of **Castelluccio** (actually just over the border in Umbria). The route also passes close under the peak of **Monte Vettore**, the Marche's highest mountain.

But the tour is not just wild mountains. Along the way there are some beguiling small towns that each boast some real architectural gem. Best of all is friendly but remote **Visso** waiting to be discovered by the more adventurous tourist.

Sarnano is a handsome town with an even more handsome backdrop of snowy peaks. With a reasonable selection of hotels and guesthouses, it makes an good base camp for this tour.

Some of the villages along the route have petrol stations but you are well advised to fill up before setting out. During winter months, though the roads are usually kept clear, you must have snow chains on board if you are driving the highest stretches. During the summer carry a bottle or two of mineral water and a good pair of hiking boots to strike off on foot into the mountains.

The Route

Part I - Sarnano to Bolognola

Sarnano lies along the main SS.78, roughly half way between the two provincial capitals of Macerata and Ascoli Piceno. For full details on the town see page 113.

The tour heads off up into the mountains above Sarnano. From Piazza della Libertà, in the modern part of the town, follow the signs for Sasso Tetto. A good wide road winds up the mountain slopes, through coppiced beech woods and limestone crags until, after about twelve kilometres, it reaches **Sasso Tetto**, one of the Marche's main ski resorts, and well equipped with ski lifts and accommodation.

Continuing on, the road rises to the Meta Pass before dropping to **Bolognola.** At 1,070 metres, Bolognola has the distinction of being the highest village in the Marche as well as the smallest council district, with only 176 inhabitants to govern. This remote hideaway was founded in the 13th century by three families who fled from Bologna during the wars between the papal Guelphs and the supporters of the Holy Roman Emperor, the Ghibellines.

Part II - Bolognola to Visso

Continuing onwards, the road drops gently down through **Acquacanina** - the beautiful Parish Church of Santa Maria di Rio Sacro on the right was founded by the Benedictines around the year 1000 and contains several noteworthy paintings - and on to **Fiastra**. Here, the artificial lake, a haven for fishermen and windsurfers, stretches for over four kilometres along the valley of the River Fiastrone. Bear left and up towards the village, passing the ruins of an 11th century castle on a pine-clad hillock to the right of the road. It was the home of the ruling Malagotti family in the 1400s. A century later, Benedictine monks used the site to build the church of San Paolo whose slim tower rises up from within the ruins.

Leaving the mountains behind for a while, we drive through a more gentle landscape of pocket-handkerchief fields squeezed between wooded hillocks until we arrive at **Pievebovigliana.** Stop here to admire the fine romanesque parish church of Santa Maria Assunta. It sits on a hillock, at the centre of the original settlement and above the more recent village. Inside the perfectly preserved 12th century romanesque exterior, an 18th century priest decided to modernize the place with a neo-classical refit. Fortunately, he didn't get as far as the beautiful crypt. Like many early churches, it was built using materials from ancient Roman times. The vaulted roof is supported by Roman pillars and a doorway has been blocked up with a 2nd century stone tablet.

Driving onwards towards the main SS.77, note the slim bridge which used to carry the road over the River Chienti - it stands to the right of the present road, just before the junction. Here again, the foundations go back to the Roman period. Heading west along the main road, we leave it after just over a kilometre to turn south along the SS.209, passing **Pieve Torina** (whose own romanesque church was badly knocked about by the 1997 earthquake) and enter the wood-flanked Valnerina valley.

Shortly before arriving at Visso take a short detour to visit the **Sanctuary of Macereto**, a perfectly symmetrical jewel of a Renaissance church built 1,000 metres up on a high plateau in 1529. An atmospheric sight in the wilderness.

The small but elegant town of **Visso**, a few kilometres further on, holds one of the architectural delights of the southern Marche. See page 122 for fuller details.

A detour , up the slopes of Monte Bove above Visso, takes you to the small ski resort of **Ussita,** in summertime carpeted with rare alpine flowers.

Part III - Visso to Piano Grande

From Visso, follow the signs to **Castelsantangelo sul Nera**. Here, the road begins to zigzag up until you arrive at the Nera pass. Suddenly ahead of you, at the far end of a natural basin, stands the lone village of **Castelluccio**. This cluster of houses, piled up on a rocky outcrop, is perhaps the remotest part of central Italy and stood almost abandoned until a few years ago. At first sight it seems hard to understand why it was ever built. But once you climb the last stretch of road into the village, the reason becomes apparent. On the other side, stretching out for almost ten kilometres is the oneiric sight of the **Piano Grande**.

This vast fertile plain, over 1,400 metres above sea level, is one of the most awesome natural sites in Italy and the home of another famous regional product, the lentil. The small, thin-skinned *lenticchie di Castelluccio* are sown here and harvested in late summer. Stop to experience the overwhelming silence of the place, broken only by the sound of the Castelluccio church bell - in bad weather, the bell was rung continuously until the last of the village's tiny population had returned home.

Half way across Piano Grande, the road divides. Our route takes us to the left (following signs in the direction of Ascoli Piceno). Reaching the pass at Forca di Presta the rugged southern crags of **Monte Vettore** come into view on the left. At 2,476 metres, this is the highest mountain in central Italy and will remain our constant companion for the remainder of the journey. Out ahead of us to the south stretch the Monti della Laga, the next link in the Apennine chain, in the Abruzzo region. As the road threads downwards, follow the signs for Montegallo.

Before long, signs of human habitation return. The principal livelihood of the tiny mountain communities in this area comes from coppicing the woodland slopes.

Arriving at **Balzo di Montegallo**, the mighty eastern face of Monte Vettore looms into sight. Stop at the village *belvedere* to take a closer look through the coin-operated telescope or pause in the shade of a nearby bar. Continuing down into the valley, follow the signs to Comunanza and then Montemonaco. The road snakes down and onwards under the ever-present gaze of Monte Vettore.

Passing through the village of **Montemonaco**, the road edges along a knife-edge spur before winding on to the mountain stronghold of Montefortino. Just before the village, a 15-kilometre dead-end detour takes you to the **Gola dell'Infernaccio**, an awe-inspiring gorge carved through the rock by the river Tenna, and excellent trekking territory.

Stop at **Montefortino** to wander around its picturesque narrow streets (you can drive into the village but only if you are confident that you know your car width well). The *Palazzo Municipale* houses the charming small Fortunato Duranti collection of 15th and 16th century paintings donated by a local artist during the 19th century (open weekday mornings from 10am-1pm). Just after the village, a 12-kilometre detour to the left leads along the beautiful valley of the River Ambro to the 17th century Sanctuary of the **Madonna dell'Ambro,** a place of pilgrimage since 1073, when a mute shepherdess saw an apparition of the Virgin Mary.

The route now heads for **Amandola**. Follow its main street up to the smart porticoed Piazza del Risorgimento. As you sip your *aperitivo* at one of the bars, admire the clock over the baroque Porta San Giacomo and the sunken frontage of the church of Sant'Agostino with its 15th century gothic-Venetian portal. Further up, in Piazza Umberto I, one tower is all that remains of the 14th century stronghold which protected the town. The town hall also houses a rural history museum - *Il Museo della Civiltà Contadina*. Sarnano is now just 12 kilometres away along the main SS.78.

One good tarn

Before the snow settles on the peaks of the Sibillini Mountains take an invigorating trek to see one of the region's natural wonders - the Lago di Pilato. This magical lake lies at a height of 1,900 metres and takes its name from the legend that Pontius Pilate's body was dragged here by a team of oxen after Tiberius condemned him to death. The lake is also the only place in the world where you'll find *Chirocephalus marchesonii,* a pink crustacean that swims belly up.

The hike to the lake takes around 3 hours each way and departs from the village of Foce near Montemonaco. The Parco Nazionale dei Monti Sibillini website (www.sibillini.net/) is a good place to start if you want to explore the area.

Tour 8
Ascoli and Fermo's hidden heritage

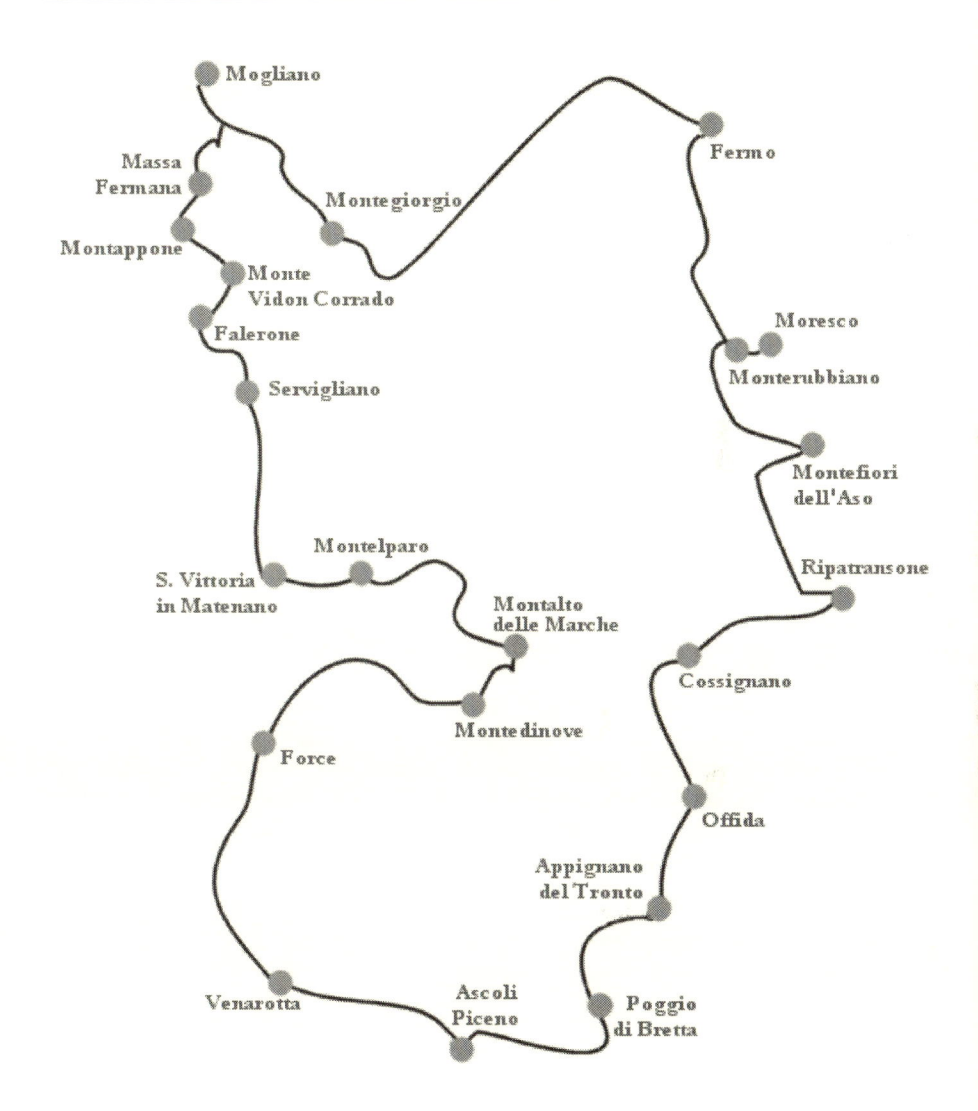

Between the Apennine mountains and the Adriatic sea, the landscape of the Marche is dominated by the towers of several hundred fortified towns and villages, sitting proudly on crests which punctuate the horizon in every direction. Most were built as feudal strongholds, each has its own particular history to tell, and many also remain surpringly unaltered by time.

Many of these southern Marche towns also conceal some remarkable works of art which can still be seen inside the buildings for which they were commissioned. Several great painters came to work in this part of the region. Two names stand out in particular. Carlo Crivelli came here from Venice in 1468 and worked here until his death in around 1493. Fifty years later, another Venetian, Lorenzo Lotto, followed in his footsteps and painted many fine masterpieces until his death at Loreto in 1556.

This tour takes in a score of fascinating towns and villages to search out just some of the region's hidden art treasures, as well as visiting a Roman amphitheatre and relics of England's St Thomas Becket along the way.

The Route

Part I - Ascoli Piceno to Offida

This tour begins in the Marche's splendid southern provincial capital, **Ascoli Piceno**, a city rich in architectural and artistic attractions. Seek out, in particular, Carlo Crivelli's magnificent panelled altarpiece of the *Madonna and Child with Saints* (1473) in the Duomo, regarded as among his finest works, and two triptychs of the *Madonna and Child with Saints* in the nearby art gallery. See page 84 for a full description of the town.

Ten kilometres east of Ascoli at **Poggio di Bretta**, the parish church contains a fresco by Crivelli which is thought to be one of his earliest works. From here, continue northwards, passing through **Appignano del Tronto** to **Offida** a fine old town famous for its hand-made lace (see page 103).

Part II - Offida to Fermo

We now cross the valley of the River Tesino towards Ripatransone, passing the walled village of **Cossignano**, teetering high up on its hilly retreat. The warm pink brick of **Ripatransone** is much the same as it has been for centuries. The first surprise is the relative grandeur of its buildings for the modest size of the town. During the 16th century it experienced a period of prosperity and prestige, and was elevated to the status of *città* with its own cathedral. The town's uniqueness, however, comes in the form of a tiny alleyway - it is only 43 centimetres wide and the narrowest in all Italy. And there are plenty of other tight lanes to explore. Passing back out of its crumbling walls, pause to admire the magnificent views of the surrounding countryside.

Continuing northwards, the tour crosses another valley to **Montefiore dell'Aso**. Parts of the collegiate church of Santa Lucia, in Piazza della Repubblica date back to the romanesque period. The main attraction here is a series of six painted panels by Carlo Crivelli in the *Polo Museale* by the church of San Francesco. The finest of these, depicting Saint Mary Magdalene, is among the artist's most beautiful images.

Crossing the valley of the Aso River, we now arrive at **Monterubbiano**. The origins of this attractive hill town can be traced back to the 3rd century BC. The small archaeological museum in the town hall in the main square has a collection of the most interesting finds. All of the town's ten churches date back to the medieval period. Don't miss the town's pretty little sister, **Moresco**, with intact medieval walls, laid out in oval form and dominated by a tall 12th century seven-sided tower and fine 14th century clock tower. Across another valley, we reach **Fermo**, one of the southern Marche's most fascinating larger towns and capital of Fermo Province. For full details of the town see page 92.

Part III - Fermo to Falerone

Climbing down from Fermo to the SS.210, we speed quickly through the light industrial sprawl of the Tenna valley for ten kilometres before returning back into some of the southern Marche's most alluring countryside. Turn northwards up to **Montegiorgio** and then follow the scenic hilly ridge towards Francavilla d'Ete. After a few kilometres turn left at the sign for Mogliano. This pretty lane weaves backwards and forwards through steep fields and neat olive groves until we reach **Mogliano**. This unassuming town strings together a series of small, red-brick squares. It has one winning attraction - search out Lorenzo Lotto's magnificent painting of the *Assumption* (1548) in the church of Santa Maria Assunta. The Venetian master had been working in the Marche for around ten years before being commissioned to paint this haunting work.

Returning southwards, we arrive after a few kilometres at **Massa Fermana**, a village which conceals another artistic jewel. Passing through the beautiful medieval gateway, flanked by a pair of porticoed buildings, we find the parish church of San Lorenzo, half way down the main street (if closed ask at town hall for access). It boasts Carlo Crivelli's earliest piece in the Marche, a magnificent work on panels of the *Madonna and Child Enthroned* (1468). There is also another work by his brother Vittore.

Continuing on towards Falerone, we pass **Montappone**, Italy's hat capital - a stop at the hat museum, or *Il Museo del Cappello*, is a must for all hatters, and shops here sell headgear for all tastes. The route then heads for **Monte Vidon Corrado** known for its excellent salami before returning to the Tenna Valley. Below the medieval village of **Falerone** lies the ancient settlement of *Falerio Picenus*, established by the Romans in 29 BC. Most of the finest archaeological treasures unearthed were either carted away by Napoleon to grace the Louvre, or are in the Vatican museums, but several villas and baths, as well as a well-restored amphitheatre (follow the signs), are worth visiting.

Part IV - Falerone to Ascoli Piceno

Our route now travels westwards along the main SS. 210 before heading south once again. Pause at **Servigliano** to visit a perfectly square-planned village. This textbook example of 18th century urban planning, feels like a little corner of someone's private vision of Utopia, with every building laid out in perfect symmetry. Driving out of the town's southern gateway, following signs to Santa Vittoria in Matenano, the road rises once more, up into open countryside, following the line of a hilly ridge with a fine panorama.

Santa Vittoria in Matenano is named after the Roman martyr whose body was brought here by monks in 930. Her magnificent marble sarcophagus, supported on two pillars, stands in the crypt of the parish church, at the far end of the town.

Passing **Montelparo** - note the cylindrical tower which once formed part of the city wall - drive down into the vine-clad Aso valley and on to the SS.433.

A 10km detour takes us to two unexpected sights - a papal palace and relics of Saint Thomas Becket. The village of **Montalto delle Marche** stands on the opposite side of the Aso Valley, just above us. When Cardinal Montalto, a farmer's son from the nearby coastal town of Grottamare, became Pope Sixtus V in 1585, he decided to elevate this tiny village where he trained as a priest to the status of Episcopal See, building a cathedral and palace which entirely upstage the little medieval hamlet above it. Work proceeded quickly but within barely five years Pope Montalto, as he was nicknamed, was dead.

The pretty village of **Montedinove,** a little further along the ridge has a delightful tiny piazza looking out over classic *marchigiano* countryside and a church which houses relics of Saint Thomas Becket. He was Archbishop of Canterbury until his murder in 1170 on the orders of Henry II and his shrine in Canterbury Cathedral became a place of pilgrimage for almost 400 years until the reformation under Henry VIII. It is claimed that English catholics, fearful of its desecration, brought his body to Europe. Relics from it now lie in a gilded glass cask in the church of San Tommaso.

Returning to the Aso Valley, we travel westwards along the SS.433 before heading south towards Ascoli Piceno, beneath the slopes of Monte dell'Ascensione. Passing through **Force** (whose traditional craft is beaten copper-ware) and on to **Venarotta,** we are soon back in Ascoli Piceno.

Beaches

Beside the seaside – a Marche beach guide

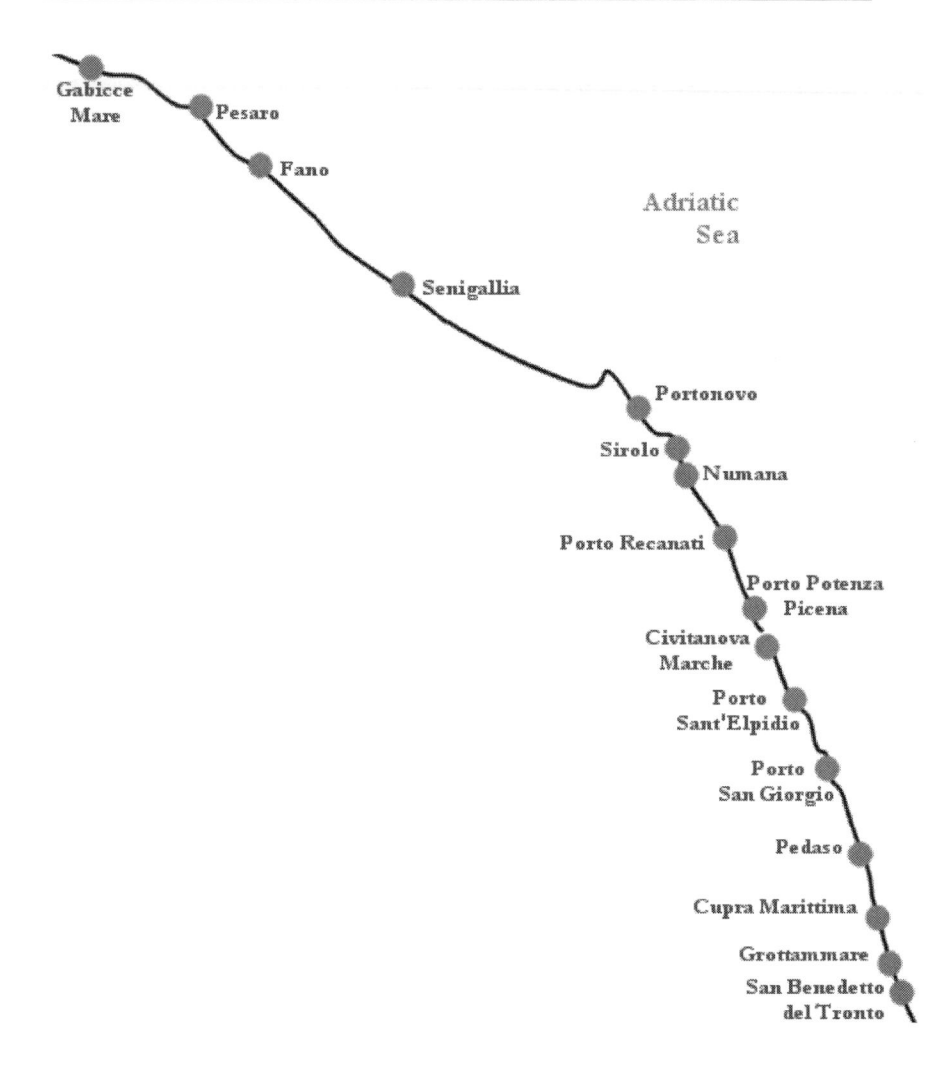

Gabicce Mare
Pesaro
Fano
Adriatic Sea
Senigallia
Portonovo
Sirolo
Numana
Porto Recanati
Porto Potenza Picena
Civitanova Marche
Porto Sant'Elpidio
Porto San Giorgio
Pedaso
Cupra Marittima
Grottammare
San Benedetto del Tronto

The Marche has around 180 kilometres of Adriatic coastline and a string of seaside resorts.

During the 1960s and '70s many of Italy's Adriatic coastal resorts saw the arrival of mass tourism which led to a precipitous and poorly-planned building boom. Sadly, this left a number of these places looking rather down-at-heel, their seafronts lined with unappealling and identical concrete hotels. However, recent attempts to smarten up these towns is paying off and many are now seeing a revival in their fortunes – and looks.

There are basically two types of beach resort in the region. First there are the bigger places with a lively atmosphere, busy night-life, plenty of visitors from abroad and a string of hotels along the promenade. Good examples include (from north to south) **Gabicce Mare**, **Pesaro**, **Fano**, **Senigallia**, and **San Benedetto del Tronto**.

Then there are the many smaller resorts with less spectacular beaches and more rented villa and apartment accommodation rather than hotels. These places are often filled for the short summer season by Italian families who faithfully return each year. The adults will always sigh that they're only there for the sake of the *bambini* but secretly love it. And there's always the mobile *telefonino* so they can pretend to be in the office. Although these beaches have less obvious charms than the bigger resorts, they are often friendly places with a certain old-fashioned charm to them.

A couple of places that don't fit into either category are the handful of resorts nestling under the lone peak of **Monte Conero**. Here you'll find rocky coves and white limestone cliffs totally unlike any other stretch of the Adriatic from Trieste in the north to the Gargano, Italy's "spur" in the south - a much more Mediterranean experience.

All the resorts in the region have a short season; basically they only feel crowded from mid-July to the third week of August. Come in mid-June or right at the end of August/early September and you'll have plenty of room with reasonably reliable weather. Most places are pretty well closed up from October through to Easter.

Although all resorts have a stretch or two of free public beach (*spiaggia libera*), it's often at the least attractive end of the strand and is rarely as clean as the pay beaches. Anyway, if you want the *real* Italian beach experience choose from one of the many pay sections with their ranks of umbrellas and sun beds. They are usually not that expensive, have all the facilities you could want and are the best place to see Italians up close. If you're staying at a resort hotel, free access to one of these beach concessions is usually included in the price.

All the places described below can be easily reached off the A14 Bologna-Pescara toll motorway. They also all lie on or near the well-served main Milano-Bari railway line.

The larger resorts have their own entry in the *Places* section of this guide; you'll find the page references below. They are ordered from north to south.

The Resorts (from north to south):

Gabicce Mare (See page 96)

Over 100 hotels, a festive atmosphere in high season and a sandy if short strand make this one of the Marche's most popular resorts.

Pesaro (See page 107)

This busy provincial capital has many other attractions apart from its fine beaches and could make a good base for exploring inland historic towns as well as lazing in the sun.

Fano (See page 91)

Plenty of space on either sandy or pebbly beaches and a beguiling old town centre with smart shops make this ancient Roman town a good all-round choice for a beach holiday.

Senigallia (See page 114)

This historic old town boasts one of the finest beaches in the Marche - 12km of velvety sand. And even if you don't want to spend all your time by the sea, it makes an interesting base for touring around the central Marche's attractive inland hill towns.

Portonovo, Sirolo, Numana (See page 102)

These three small resorts lie below the limestone peak of Monte Conero just south of Ancona and are probably the prettiest of the region's seaside places. Portonovo is the smallest while Sirolo and Numana between them have the most hotels and campsites. Given their cramped setting, they get crowded in July and August but in June and early September there's room to spare.

Porto Recanati

If you're staying inland at Loreto or Recanati, you might like to pass a day or two down here on the beach. This small-scale modern resort has an airy and spacious feel to its streets, and an attractive view of the peak of Monte Conero to the north. The beach itself is sandy gravel and rarely crowded though somewhat narrow. The most pleasant stretch is towards the north.

Porto Potenza Picena

To the north of Civitanova is Porto Potenza Picena - very much a variation on the same theme as many of the southern Marche's smaller resorts. And as the railway actually runs alongside the beach there is no room for a promenade. A place to go if you want a day on a sandy beach and you're staying nearby.

Civitanova Marche

Here, too, is a small resort that also doubles as a fishing port. Although this is a family place that will probably appeal more to tourists from nearby regions rather than foreigners, it does offer a bit more style than its neighbours. The more attractive promenade and beach lies to the south and has attractive planting and a calm air although the beach itself is gravel rather than sand.

Porto Sant'Elpidio

To the north of Porto San Giorgio is the narrow beach of Porto Sant'Elpidio. This resort's main attractions are its attractive pine woods at the northern end and plenty of enormous shoe shops on the main SS16 road (the town is in the heartland of the region's shoe industry).

Porto San Giorgio

What was once the ancient port for the inland city of Fermo is now a pleasant seaside resort with a small working port. Its streets sandwiched between the main SS16 road and the sea offer plenty of chances for window shopping, and in high summer the place has a lively air. It owes part of its charm to a few fine examples of *Liberty* style architecture that was much in vogue in the smarter seaside resorts across Italy at the opening of the 20th century.

Its 13th century fortress, built by Lorenzo Tiepolo, later Doge of Venice, stands close by the town's central square, and has fine towers and high keep. But the town's main attractions are its fish and its attractive beaches. There are plenty of moderately priced restaurants serving *brodetto* (Marche fish stew) to choose from.

Pedaso

To the south of Porto San Giorgio is Pedaso, the region's "mussel beach" - these delectable molluscs are cultivated on concrete pillars that lie just off its short, gravely beach. Apart from being a popular place for skin-diving, it is also conveniently close to the motorway exit. In summer there is also a *Sagra delle Cozze*, or mussel feast.

Cupra Marittima

An old-fashioned seaside backwater with fewer hotels and a jolly family feel - it's a place that might bring back memories of a 1950s holiday resort. Maybe it's the lush vegetation - pines, palms and oleander - that gives Cupra Marittima its relaxed charm.

Its 2.5-kilometre sandy beach, punctuated by old concrete breakwaters, complements an attractive small port, and it's rarely overcrowded. It also has a shell museum.

If you are looking to camp, the biggest sites are between here and Pedaso to the north.

Grottammare

The sandy beaches of this small resort do tend to run seamlessly into some less-attractive stretches of beach directly to the south. And although there are still plenty of palm trees, they are somehow not as grand as those at San Benedetto below. However, ignoring the ribbon-development along the SS.16 main road, its five kilometres of narrow strand are less developed than its sister and there are plenty of free public beaches. The pleasantest part is towards the centre of the town where a stretch of the promenade is pedestrian-only. The little historic *borgo* high above the main resort is also pretty and boasts some good views out to sea. Incidentally, the 43rd parallel runs right through the middle of town.

San Benedetto del Tronto (See page 111)

This is one of the main holiday resorts of the southern Marche and, with over 7,000 palm trees on its wide promenade, it has a touch of tropical charm. With plenty of hotels - some of them quite swanky - and lots of life, it makes a good base to both lie on the beach and explore old towns inland.

Keep the flags flying

Marche beaches had 25 Blue Flags in 2013 - the prestigious awards given annually to well-kept beaches and marinas across Europe by the Foundation for Environmental Education – more than any other region in Italy except for Liguria.

The important "eco-label" is given to sites that meet strict criteria including water quality, environmental management, safety and other services.

The 25 beaches and five marinas that have been nominated are in the following towns (from north to south): Gabicce Mare, Pesaro, Fano, Marotta di Mondolfo, Senigallia, Ancona, Sirolo, Numana, Porto Recanati, Potenza Picena, Civitanova Marche, Porto Sant'Elpidio, Porto San Giorgio, Cupra Marittima, Grottammare, and San Benedetto del Tronto.

Places

Ancona

The busy administrative capital of the Marche may not be an obvious destination for the average tourist. But give it time and you may well acquire a taste for the salt and spice of this restless sea port, not least for its spectacular bayside setting.

Approaching from the north you will see the city spread out on a pair of hills that form a natural amphitheatre around the harbour. Now the region's largest city, it has a notably venerable history. It was founded back in the 4th century BC by ancient Greek colonists from Syracuse in Sicily.

Later, the Romans exploited its outstanding sheltered anchorage and in AD 115, under the Roman Emperor Trajan, the present harbour walls were raised; the stately ceremonial **marble arch** – possibly the region's finest Roman monument - standing marooned at the end of the docks marks his achievement. Constructed in pale marble, the arch stands on the harbour wall itself, built on a high plinth with a travertine stone base. The limited width of the wall, which is only 11 metres wide at this point, made it necessary to create a structure which was tall but narrow so that it was clearly visible both from the land and to ships approaching the harbour from the sea.

It has a single high archway, with a height approximately two and half times its width, and is flanked on each side by two pairs of Corinthian columns. The inscription above the arch on the city side, originally in bronze letters, is dedicated to Trajan who has "given ships safer access to Italy with the construction of this port at his own expense".

The arch is depicted in a scene on Trajan's celebrated column in Rome (scene 79) where the Roman army leaves Italy to fight in the Second Dacian War.

In the southern part of the port area stands the **Mole Vanvitelliana**, or *Lazzaretto* (quarantine station) built in 1732 under the orders of Pope Clement XII by the celebrated architect Luigi Vanvitelli. This immense five-sided fortress was used to quarantine travellers coming from the Orient to prevent the spread of infectious diseases and could accommodate up to 2,000 people. It has now been restored and is used as an arts and exhibition centre.

In the Middle Ages, the forces of the German emperors, the Catholic church and the Venetian republic each made sure that Ancona was never able to establish itself as a powerful maritime republic. In 1532 it slid compliantly into the hands of the Papal States where it remained until the Unification of Italy in the 19th century.

The oldest part of town straddles **Colle Guasco**, the hill above the port. On its peak, high above the agitation of the modern city, stands Ancona's finest church and its most obvious landmark, the medieval **Cathedral of San Ciriaco**, a pleasing mix of romanesque and gothic. The austere interior is picked out with exotic Byzantine touches, a painted wooden roof in the form of an upturned boat, and a soaring 12-sided cupola - a place to linger out of the summer heat. In the crypt you can glimpse the remains of an ancient pagan temple that provided the foundation for the church.

To see the rest of the best, avoid the drab area around the railway station and start your walk from the bottom of **Corso Stamira** down by the ferry docks. After noting the Venetian-gothic facade of the ruined church of **Sant'Agostino** cut across to nearby Piazza della Repubblica where **Corso Garibaldi** and **Corso Mazzini** start (the other two *Corsi*, that complete the city's trinity of parallel main streets).

The splendidly restored 19th century **Teatro delle Muse** dominates the square. From here take a brief detour up Corso Mazzini to see the 16th century **Fontana del Calamo**, a delightful fountain with a row of 13 masked spouts.

Back down in Piazza della Repubblica, amble along Via della Loggia to see the statue-decked **Loggia dei Mercanti**, an outstanding example of florid late Venetian-gothic (the influence of Venice is never very far away here). Further on is the singular 13th century front of **Santa Maria della Piazza**, rows of blind arches and plenty of intricate carving. Inside, a glass panel in the floor allows you to see the remains of the even older church below.

From Via della Loggia walk up to **Piazza del Plebiscito** ruled over by a resplendent if cracked statue of Pope Clement XII. Over his shoulder is the neo-classical Church of **San Domenico** with a stirring **Titian *Crucifixion*** above the high altar.

As you climb up from the square on Via Pizzecolli you are in the heart of the oldest part of the city. Palazzo Bosdari at no.17 guards Ancona's **Pinacoteca**; notable paintings here include Carlo Crivelli's chilly *Madonna and Child*, Titian's *Virgin with Child and Saints*, and Lorenzo Lotto's *Sacra Conversazione*.

Further up you can rest your legs as you admire the bird's eye views of the port from Piazza Stracca. A few paces on is Palazzo Ferretti, home of the **Museo Archeologico delle Marche**, an outstanding collection of antique finds - black and red Attic vases, Etruscan bronzes, Iron Age jewellery (including some outstanding pieces from the early *Piceni* settlers).

As you wind upwards through Piazza del Senato and along Via Giovanni XXIII you will catch sight of the ruins of the Roman amphitheatre. A last effort and you are on the summit of **Colle Guasco**, with breath-taking views out to sea and the white, wind-blown face of the Cathedral behind you.

Tourist information:

via Podesti, 21
tel: 071 2225065/66/67 fax: 071 2225061
www.comune.ancona.it/

Getting there:

Ancona's Falconara Airport is served by Ryanair with daily flights from London Stansted. A regular bus service connects the airport to Ancona rail station. The city is on the main Milano-Bari railway line with frequent trains that serve most of the region's coastal towns and beyond. For drivers, the city lies off the A14 Bologna-Pescara toll motorway, exit Ancona Nord or Ancona Sud. Regular coach services from Piazza Cavour serve many of the principal inland towns (details from the tourist information office). Ancona is one of Italy's most important ferry ports serving the eastern Mediterranean and regular services run to Greece, Croatia, and Turkey.

Ascoli Piceno

Ascoli Piceno is the southern Marche's most important and alluring town - a place you can see in a day but which warrants a longer stay. It is perhaps one of central Italy's most underestimated urban centres and, along with its beautiful main square, it has other outstanding sights that manage to leave their mark on even the most blasé of tourists.

Although it is a fairly large town for the Marche with a population of some 60,000 people, the historic centre can easily be seen on foot.

Start at the **Piazza del Popolo**, the traffic-free, travertine-paved main square. This beautifully proportioned outdoor meeting place must be one of the most elegant provincial squares in all Italy. The square is the backdrop for the annual medieval tournament the **Quintana** (see below). To one side of the square stands the **Palazzo del Popolo**, a splendid 13th century building guarded over by a monumental statue of Pope Paul III. Look inside to see the arcaded Renaissance courtyard. Back in the square take a coffee with Miletti *anisette*, or aniseed-based liqueur, at the elegant **caffè Miletti**, now a historic monument and an outstanding example of Liberty style dating from 1907.

Closing off one end of the piazza is the great gothic church of **San Francesco**, a sober but pleasing building both inside and out.

The other main square, **Piazza Arringo**, is almost as impressive as its big sister and is flanked by the **Duomo**, or cathedral, and the **Palazzo Comunale**, or town hall. Inside you will find the **Pinacoteca Civica**, Ascoli's art gallery, a collection that includes some works by major artists (including two triptychs of *Madonna and Child with Saints* by Carlo Crivelli). Look, too, for the 13th century **cope** (*piviale*) of Pope Nicholas IV, a dazzling piece of old embroidery work made in England.

Inside the **Duomo** look out for the colourful painting with the *Madonna and Saints* by Carlo Crivelli (1473) which is regarded as one of the artist's finest works.

Wander round the old quarter of the town that stretches from the banks of the Tronto river to the city's main street, **Corso Mazzini** - best streets are **via Soderini** and **via di Solestà**.

Ascoli is famous across Italy for its irresistable *olive ascolane*, or deep-fried, stuffed olives. These are made from a particularly fleshy green olive grown locally that is carefully pitted, cut into a spiral, stuffed with meat and breaded before being deep fried. Try them with *crema fritta*, delicious breaded and deep-fried cubes of a sweet egg custard...naughty, yes, but very nice. To try them at their best make for Ascoli at the end of April when the town dedicates an annual festival to all things fried.

La Quintana

Ascoli's jousting tournament is one of the most authentic and exciting of these medieval shows in the Marche and takes place in the main square on the first Sunday of August. The high point of the games is when riders from the city's six districts tilt with lances at the target.

The day also includes a massive procession with around 1,400 townspeople dressed in 15th century costume and plenty of side-shows and open-air eating. Not quite as famous as the *Palio* at Siena but certainly an exciting experience.

Tourist information:

Piazza Arringo, 7
tel: 0736 298204/298334/253045 fax: 0736 298204
www.comune.ascolipiceno.it

Getting there:

Ascoli Piceno is served by train with a branch line from San Benedetto del Tronto on the main Milano-Bari railway. For drivers, the town can be reached by a motorway spur off the A14 Bologna-Pescara toll motorway.

Cagli

This courtly little town, set against a backdrop of some of the highest peaks in the northern Marche, has welcomed strangers for over two thousand years, since the days when ancient Rome made it an important staging post on the *Via Flaminia*, or Flaminian Way (one of the oldest and most important Roman roads in Europe).

Still today Cagli retains its Roman grid plan that frames a splendid **central square** with a florid fountain, a steely medieval town hall, and huddles of old men deep in gossip.

The hand of the great *Quattrocento* military architect Francesco di Giorgio is unmistakable in the dramatic oval ***Torrione*** or tower to the west of the piazza, all that remains of the citadel that Urbino's ruling Duke Federico da Montefeltro had built above Cagli towards the end of the 15th century.

Search out the pleasing fresco of the *Madonna and Child with Saints* by Giovanni Santi - the angel to the left of the picture is said to be a portrait of Santi's better known son, Raphael. You will find it in the church of **San Domenico** near the hospital.

Try to see inside the **theatre** behind the town hall, a perfect little 19th century opera house with all the trimmings and now restored to all its glory.

You might well be just as happy wandering along the medieval streets looking out for some of the many aristocratic *palazzi* that abound or lazing away a morning at a table outside one of the pleasant bars on the main square - a good place to watch everyday Italian life.

The beauty of Cagli as a town, however, is overshadowed by the natural splendour of its setting amidst some of the northern Marche's most uncontaminated **countryside**

A tortuous 10 km drive up from the town will take you to the windswept meadows 1108 metres up on the summit of **Monte Petrano**, olympian views and a mass of wild daffodils in late spring (follow signs from near the Torrione).

Tourist information:

Via Alessandri, 4
tel: 0721 780773
www.comune.cagli.ps.it

Getting there:

Cagli lies about 40 kms inland from Fano on the main SS3. There are regular coaches from the coast, Urbino and Rome.

Caldarola

This small gem of a town is inextricably linked with the fortunes of one family. The Pallotta family produced four cardinals and reached its heyday in the last decade of the 16th century when Evangelista Pallotta transformed the town to mark his elevation to Cardinal.

In Piazza Vittorio Emanuele in the centre of town stands the ***Palazzo dei cardinali Pallotta***. It was built at the end of the 1500s by Cardinal Evangelista Pallotta and now doubles as town hall and exhibition space. The magnificent ***Stanza del Paradiso***, or Hall of Paradise, completely decorated with evocative country scenes, is the most remarkable room in this elegant palace.

The splendid Collegiate Church of San Martino which stands next door also dates from this period. Several paintings inside are by members of the De Magistris family, important local painters who lived here in the 16th & 17th centuries. Chief amongst this artistic clan was **Simone De Magistris** (1538?-1613). The dream-like quality and moody mannerism of this Marche painter have lead art historians to compare him to El Greco. You can also see good examples of his work in the Church of Santi Martino e Giorgio in nearby Vestignano.

On the edge of town visit the cardinal's **castle**, Castello Pallotta, which he used as his summer residence. It is still owned by the family and now open to the public (closed Monday).

Tourist information:

P.zza Vittorio Emanuele,13
tel: 0733 903 706 fax: 0737 520225
www.comune.caldarola.mc.it/

Getting there:

Caldarola, in Macerata province, lies just off the main SS77 about 12 kms south of Tolentino.

Camerino

Poised on a ridge between two river valleys, this small but impressive town boasts not only a bishop but also a university. Its **centro storico**, or old centre, has seen relatively little change over the last few centuries, leaving it a particularly attractive sight, and the opulence of the architecture is all the more impressive for the fact that the town claims a mere 7,000 permanent residents.

The town's venerable history goes back to Neolithic times. The Romans, Goths, Byzantines and Lombards all left their imprint on the place and under Charlemagne it was made the capital of the *Marca* of Camerino.

Its heyday, however, was under the feudal lords of the Da Varano family. who in Renaissance times seemed to be related to all the great noble families of Italy. Things, though, came to an unhappy end for the last of the Da Varano rulers, Giulio Cesare - he and three of his sons were strangled in 1512 under the orders of the infamous Cesare Borgia (who Italians often call *il Valentino*).

Most of its buildings were constructed during the enlightened rule of the Da Varano through the 14th and 15th centuries when its court drew artists and scholars from across Italy.

The narrow main street takes you from the town's fortress to the principal square, **Piazza Cavour**, around which stand the Cathedral, the Archbishop's Palace and the Ducal Palace, now part of the University. Over it all watches a fine statue of Pope Sixtus V dating from 1587.

The porticoed **courtyard** of the Ducal Palace is partly attributed to the great 15th century architect Baccio Pontelli. From it leads a splendid **balcony** with great views of the Sibillini Mountains.

The grand architectural complex of San Domenico, built between the 13th and 16th centuries, has been lovingly restored and now houses a choice collection of works from the Camerino School of painting, a school described by the Italian art critic Federico Zeri as of great importance for Italian painting of the 14th and 15th centuries.

Another of Camerino's gems is the **Teatro Marchetti** off the courtyard in the Palazzo Comunale. Built in 1856, it has recently been restored and is back in use.

> **Little gems**
>
> Camerino is one of 17 Marche towns to have been awarded the Touring Club Italiano's prestigious "Orange Flag" award. The *Bandiere Arancioni Touring* are given to small inland *comuni* across Italy in recognition of the quality of what they offer the tourist.
>
> The scheme, run by Italy's leading independent tourism association, aims to give an incentive to smaller corners, away from the better known resorts and larger art towns, who take their visitors seriously. The region's winners are currently Acquaviva Picena, Camerino, Corinaldo, Genga, Gradara, Mercatello sul Metauro, Mondavio, Montecassiano, Montelupone, Monterubbiano, Ostra, Pievebovigliana, Ripatransone, San Ginesio, Sarnano, Staffolo and Urbisaglia.

Tourist information:

Palazzo Bongiovanni, Corso Vittorio Emanuele II, 17
tel: 0737 634725
www.comune.camerino.mc.it/

Getting there:

Camerino lies well inland from the coast and is reached from Macerata either on the SS361 or the SS77. It can be reached by a combination of train and bus taking the Civitanova Marche-Fabriano rail line and changing onto the connecting bus at Castelraimondo.

Cingoli

This singularly attractive central Marche walled town in Macerata province is built on a hill that receives the last rays of the sun when all around is in shadow; "*non è ancor notte a Cingoli*", (it's not yet night at Cingoli) goes a popular Marche saying, meaning "don't count your chickens before they're hatched".

The town also has the title "Balcony of the Marche" for its sweeping **panoramas** - the best views are from behind the church of San Francesco. Climb up Corso Garibaldi to **Piazza Vittorio Emanuele**, once the forum of Roman *Cingulum* and still the heart of this stone-built town.

To one side stands a fine 16th century Renaissance **town hall** with a much earlier clock tower. Inside is the smart, newly arranged **Museo Archeologico** with interesting Bronze Age finds - to see the collection call at the library (*Biblioteca comunale*) in Via Mazzini 1. The library also houses the town's **Pinacoteca**, or art gallery, with another of the Marche's serendipity paintings by Lorenzo Lotto, this time a sumptuous ***Madonna of the Rosary***.

Cingoli's brief moment of glory came with the one-year papacy of its son, Pius VIII, in 1829 - it was he who ordered a new facade for the late baroque

Cathedral on the main *piazza*, never finished due to his early death. Behind the town hall is the stern **Via del Podestà**, Cingoli's most atmospheric old street.

Tourist information:

tel: 0733 602444
www.comune.cingoli.mc.it/

Getting there:

At the very centre of the Marche, Cingoli lies on the SS502 off the main Ancona-Fabriano SS76.

Corinaldo

Although a small place, Corinaldo in Ancona province is a remarkably pretty fortified hill town. All of a medieval piece, it boasts some of the best-preserved 15th century defensive **walls** in the whole of the Marche. Walk long stretches of the battlements while admiring the sweeping **views**.

It's worth wondering up and down the narrow, stepped streets, and visiting the **shrine** to **St Maria Goretti**, the town's own 20th century saint. Born in Corinaldo in 1890, she was murdered in 1902 in Lazio – where her parents had moved for work - at the age of 12 by a would-be rapist whom she resisted. She was canonised in 1950 as a virgin martyr.

The town is on the edge of the Verdicchio wine country and the local Val di Nevola co-operative winery produces some excellent value bottles.

On the third Sunday in July the town holds an unusual festival dedicated to *polenta*, the corn meal 'porridge' that was once a peasant staple. The *Contesa del pozzo della polenta* commemorates the moment when the town's people successfully resisted a siege in 1517 thanks to copious supplies of it.

Tourist information:

Largo XVII Settembre 1860, n° 1-2
tel: 071 6793236 fax: 071-6793235
www.corinaldo.it

Getting there:

Corinaldo lies some 20 kms inland from the main coastal A14 motorway, off the SS424.

Fabriano

Fabriano in Ancona province is famed across the world for its paper. Even back in the 14th century, its medieval mills were producing a remarkable million sheets of paper a year and it was here that the watermark for paper was first used. Its paper is still used the world over for banknotes and quality art paper.

The industrial sprawl of the suburbs may not appeal much - the town is also home to one of Italy's best-known domestic appliance manufacturers. It is, however, well worth penetrating to the heart of the old town to see the opera-set main **Piazza del Comune** flanked by the gothic **Palazzo del Podestà** with swallow-tail battlements. Centre-stage is the splendid three-tiered **Sturinalto fountain**, built at the close of the 13th century.

So proud is the town of its traditional industry that it has dedicated an interesting modern museum to it - you'll find the **Museo della Carta** in the former monastery of San Domenico to the south of the town on Largo Fratelli Spacca. You can also buy hand-made Fabriano paper here.

The town was the birthplace of Gentile da Fabriano, Italy's greatest master of the late 14th century International Gothic style of painting. You will have to make do, however, with works by his followers, best of whom was Allegretto Nuzi - you can find his work in the **Pinacoteca Comunale** in tiny Piazza Umberto I behind the main square, and in the **Duomo** next door.

Also in the Duomo are handsome **frescoes** by Orazio Gentileschi, a 17th century follower of Caravaggio who ended his days as court painter to the ill-fated King Charles I of England.

Fabriano Paper

The art of paper-making arrived in Europe from China sometime around the 8th century and Fabriano was one of the earliest places in Europe to start large-scale production. Already by the 13th century a number of factories are recorded in official documents.

Many major innovations in paper-making were invented in the town and include the first use of water power to pulp the raw fibres and the replacement of old starch-based glues, which caused rapid deterioration of the paper, with animal-based gelatine glues from tannery by-products.

Fabriano is also credited with the first use of watermarks in paper, originally as a way of identifying the paper maker and the quality of the material. The earliest known watermarked Fabriano papers go back to the end of the 13th century. Later the use of watermarking at Fabriano developed into an art in its own right.

Tourist information:

Piazza del Comune, 4
tel: 0732 625067/709480 fax: 0732 629791
www.fabrianoturismo.it/

Getting there:

Fabriano is on the main Ancona-Rome rail line. By car it is best reached on the main SS76 road from Ancona.

Fano

Fano is an unassuming but lively seaside resort, a busy fishing port and an ancient town with a beguiling old centre. With a population of nearly 64,000 it is the third largest town in the Marche, but retains a feeling of intimacy.

The Roman colony of *Fanum Fortunae* took its name from a noted temple to the goddess of Fortune that once stood here. Still today Fortune reigns, but in the Christian guise of one of the town's patron saints, San Fortunato. In Roman times the place was both an important port and cross-road where the ancient *Via Flaminia* from Rome met the coastal route heading north.

The **Arco di Augusto**, a splendid white stone Roman triumphal arch, provides a fitting gateway to the town. It was completed in AD 10 under orders of the Roman Emperor Augustus as part of his ambitious project to modernise one of the Empire's most important strategic highways. The via Flaminia, or Flaminian Way, running from Rome to Rimini, had been built by the Roman Consul Gaius Flaminius in 220 BC to carry Rome's great armies to the northern reaches of the Empire. The arch was originally flanked by two circular towers, of which only one survives. On either side of the main six-metre wide archway are two smaller arches.

In the fourth century the arch was briefly re-dedicated to Constantine the Great and a seven-arched portico was added to the top. This was partially destroyed when Federico da Montefeltro, Duke of Urbino, lay siege to the city in the 15th century - the remains of two columns can still be seen today. On the wall of the church on the right outside the arch is a 16th century bas-relief showing the arch as it was originally built.

From here the main **Via Arco di Augusto** sets a course through the old centre (if you keep following the road it will eventually take you across the railway tracks to finish on the stony Sassonia beach).

At the main cross-road in the centre turn right up **Corso Matteotti** to arrive at central **Piazza XX Settembre** decorated with a whimsical 16th century fountain topped by the goddess Fortune. The arcaded **Teatro della Fortuna**, standing to one side, is the town's recently restored 19th century theatre - an excellent example of the miniature opera-house style stuccoed theatres that dot the Marche.

The other notable building that flanks the square is the **Palazzo Malatesta**. The palace holds the town's **Museo Civico** and **Pinacoteca**, a mixed collection including some fine Renaissance medals and paintings by Guercino, Guido Reni and Michele Giambono.

The striking courtyard and loggia of the palace, known as the **Corte Malatestiana**, hosts open-air concerts in high summer.

The church of **Santa Maria Nuova**, just off the main square on Via de Pili, holds two treasures by **Perugino**, a *Madonna with Saints* and an *Annunciation* - it is probable that the young Raphael helped the Umbrian master with the former picture.

The town has a particularly elegant *passeggiata* - that uniquely Italian communal early evening stroll - along the town's main streets flanked by tempting shops.

The railway cleanly splits the old town from the modern resort that has grown up along two stretches of fine beach. To the south-east runs the **Spiaggia Sassonia**, a long strand of pebbly beach with a wide promenade. To the north-west runs the shorter **Spiaggia Lido**, all sand and serried rows of beach umbrellas - the busier of the two.

Between the two beaches lies the fishing **harbour** with a shop selling the best from the freshly-landed catch - the *vongole* or baby clams are particularly good.

Both north and south of Fano run pleasant enough **beaches**, often relatively uncrowded and with a few stretches of public sands (*spiaggia libera*) where you don't have to pay.

Tourist information:

via C.Battisti, 10
tel: 0721 803534
www.turismofano.com/

Getting there:

Fano, in Pesaro & Urbino province, is on the main Milano-Bari railway line with frequent trains that serve most of the region's coastal towns and beyond. For drivers, the town lies off the A14 Bologna-Pescara toll motorway, exit Fano, and at the end of the ancient *Via Flaminia*, now the SS3.

Fermo

A venerable old hill town with a lively feel, Fermo boasts an ensemble of architectural sights which make it well worth a visit. Since 2009 it has also been the main town in the region's new province of Fermo.

Starting at the highest part of the town, the fortress which once topped the place was destroyed in 1445 in a popular rebellion against the ruling Sforza family and is now the site of municipal gardens which afford good **views** over the *marchigiano* countryside (and a spacious car park).

The nearby 13th century romanesque-gothic **cathedral**, with its richly decorated interior and fine rose window, now stands in splendid isolation. For British visitors, perhaps the most interesting of the cathedral's treasures is a cope said to have belonged to St Thomas Becket, Archbishop of Canterbury (1118-1170) and a masterpiece of early Arabic embroidery, on display in the excellent *Museo Diocesano* adjacent to the church.

The main town stands on a level just below the cathedral. Built around the magnificent large square, the **Piazza del Popolo**, are the main municipal buildings. Sansovino's grand statue (1590) of the bishop of Fermo who was to become Pope Sixtus V tops the main entrance of the **Palazzo Comunale** which contains the town's art collection, in which the most notable work is an early Rubens painting of the *Nativity* (1608).

During the summer period the *piazza* plays host to Fermo's music festival featuring some of the world's finest performers, as well as outdoor markets.

Also worthy of note are the underground **piscine romane** (roman pools), thirty magnificently preserved underground chambers built between 41 and 60 BC to supply the town's water, that are regarded as the finest example of their kind in Italy.

Tourist information:

Piazza del Popolo, 5
tel: 0734 228738
www.turismo.fermo.net/

Getting there:

Fermo stands just inland from the main coastal A14 motorway on the SS210. There is a regular bus service from Porto San Giorgio by the sea.

Fossombrone

This small town, once the Roman settlement of *Forum Sempronii*, looks splendid from afar on the slopes of the valley of the Metauro river.

Church towers and the upper storeys of larger noble palaces peep out through the terracotta roofs of the town's terraced streets, while above stands the 15th century Corte Alta *palazzo*, now home to an interesting **civic museum** and art gallery.

Higher still loom the ruins of the medieval bastion built by the Malatesta family, lords of Fano, to defend the town against their rivals, the Montefeltro of Urbino.

Most of the buildings, however, date from the period after its conquest by Federico da Montefeltro, Duke of Urbino, when the town saw its period of greatest prosperity - the finest of these are the gracious but modest Renaissance *palazzi* along a pair of parallel **arcaded streets** in the centre of the town.

A short distance from the centre, along the ancient *via Flaminia*, are the remains of the ancient settlement of **Forum Sempronii**, named after the plebeian tribune Gaius Sempronius Gracco who built the forum between 133 and 126 BC. The town was laid out on a grid-like plan which ran parallel with the Flaminian Way. Excavations have brought to light the remains of a *domus*, or family house, with a thermal heating system, and a long stretch of basalt paving running parallel to the Flaminian Way.

Other archaeological finds are displayed in the Civic Museum in the Corte Alta *Palazzo* above the town.

Tourist information:

Piazza Dante
tel: 0721 716324
www.montefeltro.info/

Getting there:

Fossombrone, in Pesaro & Urbino province, is around 30 kms inland from Fano on the main SS3 from where it can be reached by a regular bus service.

Frasassi Caves

The region's limestone mountains are riddled with caves, many of which are a paradise for pot-holers. But none compare with the **Grotte di Frasassi**, one of Italy's largest and most famous complexes of caves that start from the dramatic Frasassi Gorge.

Some 13 kilometres of limestone caverns have so far been explored, and it is reckoned that they may run for up to 35 kms. Only one and a half kms of this crystalline wonderland is open to the general public. Equipped with walkways and theatrical lighting, it includes the awesome **Grotta Grande del Vento**, Europe's largest single cavern, so vast that Milan Cathedral would fit comfortably inside, and some of the most extravagantly fanciful stalagmites and stalactites you are ever likely to see. Even claustrophobics shouldn't find it too challenging. And it's an ideal jaunt for a rainy day.

The guided tour lasts around an hour; dress up warmly as the temperature inside is a constantly low 14° C. Be warned, however that it can get quite crowded in high summer, especially at weekends.

Even if you don't have time to see the caves, stop to admire the splendid backdrop of the **Frasassi Gorge** and the romanesque **church** in the little spa of **San Vittore delle Chiuse**. This tiny, perfectly square *chiesetta* was built in the 12th century on chastely simple lines and is one of the prettiest of its kind in the Marche.

Further up the gorge a slowly climbing footpath leads up to the remarkable octagonal church known as the **Tempio del Valadier,** a perfect Neoclassical building in creamy travertine tucked in a cave high up on the walls of the gorge. It was built in 1828 by the celebrated Roman architect Giuseppe Valadier - one of Italy's leading exponents of Neoclassicism - under the orders of Pope Leo XII who was born in the nearby village of Genga in 1760.

Caves Information: The car park, where you must buy your tickets, is some distance away from the actual cave entrance which is served by a minibus. English and German tours are available. For opening times, ticket prices and other information visit www.frassasi.com or telephone 0732 90090/90080.

Getting there:

Frasassi is just of the main Ancona-Fabriano SS76 road. There is also a nearby rail station at Genga on the Rome-Ancona line.

Furlo Gorge

If you're travelling along the modern SS3 *superstrada* turn off at the signs for **Furlo** rather than taking the 3 km tunnel on the main road. You will now be on the ancient **Roman Via Flaminia** and in for a treat as you drive through the gorge.

This is a place for lovers of gothic scenery. Sheer naked limestone cliffs rise up on either side of the bright green waters of the Candigliano river, leaving just enough room for the narrow road to pass.

The Flaminian Way, built by the Roman Consul Gaius Flaminius in 220 BC, was one of Ancient Rome's most important highways, used by its great armies marching to the northern reaches of the Empire. From Rome it headed north through the Apennine mountains before reaching the Adriatic coast at Fano and on to Rimini.

The narrow Furlo Gorge, 35 kms south-west of Fano, posed one of the greatest engineering challenges along the way. Huge square blocks of stone had to be used to build the road with tapered buttress supports to a height of more than 50 metres above the river as far as a rocky spur, through which a narrow tunnel was hewn by hand.

Improvement works were carried out along the road in AD 76, during the reign of the Emperor Vespasian, when a second larger tunnel, 38 metres long, was cut through the rock at the side of the original tunnel - chisel marks can still be seen in the rock today. This larger tunnel is still used by modern traffic travelling along the road.

The magnitude of this construction feat is now mostly hidden by a modern dam which has partially submerged the support walls of the road.

The small village of Furlo at the mouth of the gorge is a good place to eat truffles in season. Or you might hunt out a picnic spot by taking the **strada panoramica** from the village and climb up to the top of the gorge. But be warned - it's a longish and twisting drive.

The area is now a **nature park** and home to rare flora and fauna; you may even see a golden eagle wheeling overhead. If you're coming from the west, the gorge ends abruptly as the road enters a wide, wooded valley where the Candigliano flows into the Metauro river.

Getting there:

Furlo lies about 35 kms inland from Fano just off the main SS3, between Fossombrone and Acqualagna - follow signs for "Gola di Furlo" or "Furlo".

Gabicce & Gradara Castle

Driving on the A14 motorway you see the square towers of **Gradara castle** just by the Marche border with Emilia-Romagna. And as it's only a short coach trip away from the Adriatic beach resorts, Gradara vies with the nearby Republic of San Marino as one of the most popular day-trip destinations for the riviera package tourists.

The imposing 14th century **walls** which enclose the town (some of the best preserved in the region), with their battlements and bristling towers, are one of the most attractive landmarks to be seen from the northern Marche coastal strip.

From the car park, the single main street heads gently up through the city gates to the **fortress** at the higher end of the town, passing every type of tourist shop, stocked with schlock souvenirs to suit every age.

The castle was owned by the ruling Malatesta family. It was here, according to tradition, that Francesca da Rimini and her lover Paolo, immortalised by Dante, were murdered in 1289 (see facing page).

The Malatesta family managed to keep hold of Gradara for almost two more centuries, successfully defending it for forty-two days against a siege waged by the rival Sforza family (led by Federico da Montefeltro, the Duke of Urbino) before losing it to them in 1464.

Most of the **decoration** of the castle was carried out in 1493 by Giovanni Sforza for his young bride, the notorious Lucrezia Borgia, daughter of Pope Alexander VI and sister of the infamous Cesare. The **chapel** boasts a magnificent glazed terracotta altarpiece by **Andrea della Robbia**.

> **Francesca da Rimini**
>
> Francesca was the daughter of Giovanni da Polenta, lord of Ravenna. Gianciotto, a courageous but exceedingly ugly soldier, obtained her father's consent to marry her. Fearing that she would be repelled by his ugliness he persuaded his handsome brother Paolo to court her on his behalf, posing as Gianciotto.
>
> Once the marriage contract was signed, the real Gianciotto (the ugly one) slipped into the marriage bed, to the understandable horror of the young bride. But, more tragic still, Paolo and Francesca had fallen in love. When Gianciotto discovered that his brother had betrayed him, he murdered them both...and that is where the story would have ended, if Dante hadn't put it into the fifth *canto* of *The Inferno*.

Down by the coast below Gradara lies **Gabicce Mare**. This colourful, party-party resort on the border with Emilia-Romagna is really just an extension of the Rimini Riviera to the north. So it is not surprising that it is one of the Marche's busiest beach holiday spots with over a hundred hotels.

Still its sandy but short strand is inviting and there is a lively night life both down by the sea and up above in **Gabicce Monte** where you'll find a couple of the Adriatic's most famous night clubs and great **views** out to sea.

Heading south from Gabicce by car, follow the *strada panoramica* that heads for Pesaro passing through the **Monte San Bartolo Regional Park**. Along the winding coast road you'll have impressive views and a handful of charming coves and good-value fish restaurants, among them the intimate little port at Baia Vallugola.

Tourist information:

Piazza V Novembre, 1
tel: 0541 964115 fax: 0541 823035
www.gradara.org

Getting there:

The nearest station for both Gabicce and Gradara is Cattolica on the main Milano-Bari railway line with frequent trains that serve most of the region's coastal towns and beyond. For drivers, the town lies on the A14 Bologna-Pescara toll motorway, exit Cattolica.

Jesi

This thriving and elegant town boasts a sophisticated old centre that should not be missed. Sometimes known as the "Milan of the Marche", it also has a lively cultural life.

Its most striking feature greets you as you arrive - a belt of massive 14th century walls, built on Roman foundations, strengthened with buttresses and impregnable towers, and topped by houses. The main streets of the walled historic centre run along a narrow ridge and there is much to tempt you to explore.

Start in **Piazza Federico II** which lies at the north-eastern end of town where the Roman forum of *Aesis* once lay. The name of the square recalls the birth here of the celebrated medieval Hohenstaufen Emperor Frederick II in a tent on 26 December 1194. Frederick, known as *Stupor Mundi* for his stirring deeds, endeared himself even more to the city when he later called it his special city, "its very name seeming to recall that of Jesus". The 18th century face of the **Duomo**, the robust caryatids on the palace to the left of the church and the obelisk in the centre give the square a decidedly late baroque tone.

A few steps down Via Pergolesi and you will be in Piazza Colocci and in front of Jesi's most handsome building, the **Palazzo della Signoria**. This text-book Renaissance palace was built at the end of the 15th century by Francesco di Giorgio Martini, the Sienese genius best known for his military architecture. The large rampant lion above the entrance is the symbol of the power the city once held. Inside note the three-tiered courtyard with brick piers on the first level, marble on the second and wood on the third.

Carry on along Via Pergolesi to **Piazza della Repubblica**; Jesi's largest square is dominated by the town's 18th century theatre, **Teatro Pergolesi**, home to an interesting autumn opera season and named after the composer Giovanni Battista Pergolesi who was born here in 1710.

From here, the long main **Corso Matteotti** runs straight as an arrow to an arch built in honour of Pope Clement XII in 1734. Stroll down the street in the early evening, seemingly with half the town's population, for a most civilised *passeggiata*, or communal stroll.

On parallel Via XV Settembre stands Jesi's most flamboyant building, **Palazzo Pianetti**. Apart from its hundred windows, the bland facade little prepares you for the over-the-top rococo flourishes inside. The most extravagant part is the sugar-candy stucco work in the long *galleria*. This over-blown decoration alone would merit a visit; but the added bonus of the civic **art gallery** (*Pinacoteca Comunale*) makes it obligatory - here you'll find a small group of some of **Lorenzo Lotto's** finest works - The *Judgement of Santa Lucia*, a *Visitation*, an *Annunciation* and a restless *Deposition*.

Giovanni Battista Pergolesi

One of Italy's great baroque composers, Pergolesi was born in Jesi in 1710 but made his name at the Court of Naples where he wrote many sacred dramas, cantatas and serenatas. But his lasting fame was as a composer of opera *buffa*, or comic opera, the most famous of which was *La Serva Padrona* (1733).

His life was dogged by ill health which forced him to retire to the Franciscan Monastery at Pozzuoli where he wrote his celebrated *Stabat Mater* and *Salve Regina*. He died there in 1736, at the age of 26.

Tourist information:

Piazza della Repubblica, 9
tel:0731 538420 fax: 0731 538512
www.comune.jesi.an.it/

Getting there:

Jesi, in Ancona province, lies just off the main SS76 Ancona-Fabriano road. It is also on the main Ancona-Roma rail line.

Loreto

The striking hill town of Loreto lies just inland from the Adriatic Sea and is one of the world's most important shrines to the Virgin Mary. The town mainly exists to service the thousands of Roman Catholic pilgrims who travel here from around the world.

The great dome of the **Sanctuario della Santa Casa** dominates the countryside for miles around; below it stands the focus of worship - the **Holy House,** the rustic cottage from Nazareth that witnessed the Annunciation and the childhood of Jesus (see the story of the Holy House below).

Although the *Santa Casa* arrived, according to tradition, in 1294, it was not until 1507 that the Catholic church officially approved of Loreto as a place of pilgrimage, though work on the church had begun in 1468. It was Pope Julius II who decided to pull out all the stops and give the simple cottage a fit setting.

The result is a showcase of fine work by many of the most celebrated names of late Renaissance Italy and gives even the unbeliever good reason to come here. Started on gothic lines, later architects, including Bramante and Sansovino, gave the church a thorough late Renaissance treatment.

Inside, under the dome, is the great marble facing that protects the Holy House, carried out in the 16th century to Bramante's designs by the noted medal-designer Gian Cristoforo Romano, Andrea Sansovino and Antonio da Sangallo the Younger. Note how around its base centuries of kneeling pilgrims have worn furrows in the marble.

The curious statue within the walls of the *Santa Casa* of the black **Madonna of Loreto** is a modern copy of the original, destroyed in a fire in 1921. Some claim that the presence of black Madonnas in many famous shrines is a prophetic reference to Mary in the Song of Solomon, "I am black, but comely"; others more prosaically point out that the statues were often carved in dark hardwoods, later further blackened by the smoke of votive candles.

At the bottom of the right nave are the church's greatest **artistic treasurers** - gem-stone coloured **frescoes** in the Sacristy of St Mark by Melozzo da Forlì, and Luca Signorelli's noble frescoes in the nearby Sacristy of St John. **Piazza della Madonna**, the elegant set-piece square with a delicate baroque fountain that fronts the sanctuary is flanked on two sides by the arcades of the 16th century **Palazzo Apostolico**.

The **Museo-Pinacoteca** inside preserves a fine group of late works by **Lorenzo Lotto** (the Venetian master retired and died in the monastery here in 1556) and an unusual collection of Renaissance ceramic chemical jars.

The Legend of the Holy House

The simple cottage at Nazareth where the Annunciation took place and where the Holy Family lived, so tradition relates, was borne away by angels in 1291 as the Saracens descended on the Holy Land.

It first arrived on a hill in Dalmatia. Here it stayed until the 10th of December 1294, when it was again miraculously moved, this time across the Adriatic Sea to a laurel grove (Latin *lauretum*, hence Loreto) infested by bandits.

Its final resting place, though, was a few miles away in the middle of a public highway on the top of the hill of Loreto. Experts in our more sceptical age now suggest that the bricks of Mary's house were brought from Palestine in the ships of the retreating Crusaders, possibly by a Byzantine family named *Angeli*.

To mark the anniversary of the "Holy Translation", the *marchigiani* to this day still light large bonfires on the night between the 9 and 10 December in the open country and on the beaches to help guide the angels on their way.

The *Festa della Venuta*, as it is known, is also marked in the Basilica of Loreto with a procession where the statue of the Madonna is borne on the shoulders of airline pilots, for whom Our Lady of Loreto is the patron saint.

Tourist information:

via Solari, 3
tel: 071 970276 fax: 071 970020
http://www.santuarioloreto.it/

Getting there:

Loreto is a short drive off the main A14 toll motorway, exit Loreto. There is also a regular bus service from Ancona. Loreto's railway station to the east of the town is on the main Milano-Bari line.

Macerata

Known across the world for its annual open-air opera festival, Macerata is a human-scaled provincial capital that also warrants a visit for its other charms.

The **opera festival** in July and August has found an international following and takes place in the 7,000-seater **Sferisterio** - a monster of a Neo-classical open-air arena erected by private subscription in the 1820s. As you swoon to a Verdi aria, you might care to remember that it was originally built as a stadium for *pallone col bracciale*, an old-style form of handball.

The centre has a measured dignity fitting the place's solid, unostentatious wealth. Its centre was almost entirely built between the 16th and 19th centuries. The Renaissance two-tiered arcades of the **Loggia dei Mercanti** on the central **Piazza della Libertà** is the town's most striking piece of architecture.

The best of the city's palaces line **Corso Matteotti**, the road that leaves the square at the side of the Loggia, while **Corso della Repubblica** will take you to Piazza Vittorio Veneto and the civic **gallery and museum**. Here is a mixed bag of works by *umbro-marchigiani* painters - most important is Carlo Crivelli's *Madonna and Child*.

If you have time, you might like to examine the old carriages in the **Museo delle Carrozze** or brush up your modern Italian history in one of the country's best museums dedicated to the Unification of Italy and wartime resistance - you'll find them in the same *palazzo* as the pictures.

Helvia Ricina

The remains of the Roman city of *Helvia Recina* lie on the banks of the River Potenza, just north of Macerata. The ruins of its large amphitheatre, with a diameter of 72 metres, can still be seen today, though much of the stone was plundered in later centuries for the construction of buildings in the surrounding area. It is thought to have been built around the 2nd century AD, though some scholars date it from an earlier time, perhaps from the Augustan period. Other remains include a water tank, tombs and a stretch of paved road.

A number of stone blocks have been recovered from the river where they were probably used during the late Roman period for strengthening its banks. Several of these are decorated with inscriptions, spiral scrolls, festoons and masks and probably came from other monuments in the city.

Helvia Ricina was destroyed by the Visigoths in the 5th-6th century, forcing its inhabitants to move up to the safety of nearby hills, where they founded the cities of Macerata and Recanati.

Tourist information:

piazza della Libertà 9 – 12
tel: 0733 234807 fax: 0733 266631
www.comune.macerata.it/
www.sferisterio.it/

Getting there:
Macerata is served by the Civitanova Marche-Fabriano branch line off the main Milano-Bari rail line. By car it is some 20 kms inland off the A14 motorway, exit Macerata.

Monte Conero & its resorts

Solitary Monte Conero, just south of Ancona, provides the only really **rugged coastline** in the Marche and rises sharply out of the sea to a height of over 570 metres. The steep sides of this limestone peak slide down to the shore and the prettiest beaches on the whole of the northern Adriatic shores.

Along with its three romantic small beach resorts, the mountain has slopes clothed with dense Mediterranean *macchia*, or shrub. In recent years the whole area has been declared a regional **nature park** (see below).

Portonovo is the smallest retreat on the Conero Riviera. Admire the picture postcard views out to sea as you wind down the dead-end road to this collection of hotels, restaurants, campsites and beach huts on a narrow strip of beach. The strand is split in two by the **Fortino Napoleonico**, a squat, blank-eyed fort built in 1808 by Napoleon's Italian viceroy to fight off English ships; it is now an unusual hotel.

At the end of the road, where the evergreen oaks that smother the mountain come down to the sea, stands the early romanesque **church of Santa Maria**. Built between 1034 and 1048, its curious form is unique in Italy and looks as if it might be more at home in Normandy.

Back on the main road, the Conero trail skirts the base of the mountain with sweeping views inland. Around 8 km south from the junction for Portonovo, follow signs for Monte Conero to drive up to **Badia di San Pietro**, built in the 12th century as a Benedictine hermitage and now a hotel. This is the highest point on the mountain reachable by car and worth the journey for the **views**.

The southern spur of Conero shelters the riviera's two chief resorts. **Sirolo** is the most attractive, with a spruce medieval centre and a tree-lined, balcony *piazza* that teeters high above the sea. The best beaches are accessible using a half-hourly bus service that drops down to each of the coves.

The string of campsites and hotels below the old town runs seamlessly into more of the same at **Numana**. It has a fine long beach to the south and a small archaeological museum documenting the history of the Piceni tribes who lived here until Rome muscled in (Via La Fenice, 4).

The beauty of the Conero Riviera means that its three small resorts are crowded in July and August; come in late May, early September or, best of all, June. To escape from the crowds in high season make for one of the many small isolated coves only reachable by boat - regular services from Numana, Sirolo and Portonovo.

Inland, you might like to explore the vineyards that produce one of the Marche's finest red wines, Rosso Conero. A well-signposted wine trail winds through the backroads taking you to the *cantine* of individual producers with plenty of chances to taste and buy their wines.

Conero Regional Park

The whole area of Monte Conero was declared a regional nature park in 1987 and a web of signed footpaths cover the peak - maps and information from the *Consorzio del Parco del Conero* at Sirolo. On the summit (572 m) traces of a Palaeolithic settlement dating back some 100,000 years have been discovered - the earliest signs of human habitation in the region.

Its position half way up the Italian peninsula has made it an important zone for many species of both northern and southern European maritime flora, including rarities like *Bellevalia dubia*, *Fumana arabica* and *Aspodeline liburnica*. The park boasts over a thousand species of wild plants, as well as a rich bird life. And the views over the sea are breathtaking.

Tourist information:

P.zza Vittorio Veneto, Sirolo
tel: 071 9330611 fax: 071 9338098
http://www.rivieradelconero.info/

Getting there:

Monte Conero lies between the sea and the main A14 motorway, exit Ancona Sud. Regular bus services from Ancona.

Offida

The beguiling hill town of **Offida** is one the southern Marche's smaller gems. The old centre stands nobly on its own plug of rock, neatly separated from the modern part of town. The place still has an old-fashioned air about it and little has yet been over-restored. Although it's fun to visit when the busy Thursday market is in full swing, you'll have to park some distance from the centre. First stop is the unusual triangular main *piazza* dominated by the beautiful **town hall** - one of the finest examples of 15th century civic architecture in the Marche. The building's lovely upper loggia and swallowtail battlements give the square true class.

The church of **Santa Maria della Rocca** stands a little way from the main *piazza*, along via Roma. The romanesque gothic church is one of the area's most important examples of Piceno monastic art. It is striking, above all, for its imposing austerity, made all the more powerful by its position overlooking the city and the surrounding hills. The present building dates back to 1330 and provides clear evidence of the peculiarity of Piceno monastic style, which is marked by simplicity and an almost total absence of decoration. The upper church, with its single, notably high nave and truss-beam ceiling, is reached by a spiral staircase. Note the restored 14th century frescoes in the apse. The altar is also interesting - it is made from a stone sarcophagus from the Roman period and carved with dancers and bunches of grapes.

Back in the town centre, a web of narrow alleyways invitingly beckon you to explore - look out for the numerous Renaissance details while you wander about. Then to round off a visit you could always buy some of the hand-made lace - *pizzo a mano* - that the town is famous for (see below). You'll find a number of shops selling it.

Offida has an unusual carnival celebration on Shrove Tuesday when bundles of canes stuffed with straw - known as *i vlurd* - are lit and taken in a flaming procession round the streets before being added to a giant bonfire in the main piazza.

Offida Lace

Lace making is one of the most common crafts practised by the women of Offida. They can still be seen, seated at their doorways in old town passageways, working intently, often with great rapidity, with bobbins, threads of white or grey yarn and pins on designs of flowers and animals. Originally begun among working families in the 1400s, the art of pillow-lace making was later cultivated by religious orders and aristocratic families. It was the Benedictine nuns who encouraged the spread of this art, which led to an increase in production during the second half of the 1600s. In 1979, the Offida Craft Lace Co-operative was set up to encourage the production of Offida lace and to sell it directly to the customer. There is also an annual *Mostra e Mercato del Merletto* in mid-July with both lacy and culinary delights to tempt you.

Tourist information:

tel: 0736 88871 fax: 0736 889648
www.turismoffida.it/

Getting there:

Offida, in Ascoli Piceno province, lies some 20 kms inland from San Benedetto del Tronto on the coast. There are buses from both San Benedetto and Ascoli Piceno.

Osimo

The town's compact, warm brick *centro storico* rides the crest of a hill above the more modern town expansion below. Most of its best buildings date from the 17th and 18th centuries but signs of its ancient past sometimes show through.

Drop into the entrance hall of the **Palazzo Comunale** in main **Piazza del Comune** to see a dozen **statues** from Roman *Auximum*, as the place was called in ancient times, and hunt out the sturdy blocks of the **Roman walls** above Via Fonte Magna. The street plan of the old town still retains its Roman layout.

The **mosaic pavement** of the Duomo is a fine relic of medieval times. The old romanesque **church of San Francesco** has been smothered inside and out in high baroque to celebrate its later reincarnation as the **sanctuary** dedicated to San Giuseppe da Copertino (1603-1663) (see below).

Osimo also boasts a mysterious "underground city", a warren of **caverns and passageways** carved in the soft rock under the historic centre and decorated with mysterious religious and alchemical symbols. Part of them have been restored and atmospherically lit and are open to the public.

St Joseph of Copertino

San Giuseppe da Copertino is known as the patron saint of those undergoing exams. Thanks also to his celebrated capacity for levitation, he is also much invoked in the U.S.A as a protector of pilots.

Born in 1603 in Salento in Southern Italy, after overcoming failure in his studies (hence his role for students) he became a wandering Franciscan friar. He finally settled in the friary in Osimo where he died six years later in 1663.

His remains are kept in a crystal urn in the modern crypt. You can also see the rooms, known as the *camere di San Giuseppe* where in religious rapture he is said to have levitated.

Tourist information:

Via Fonte Magna 12
tel: 071 7236088 fax: 071 7231554
www.comune.osimo.an.it/

Getting there:

Osimo is best approached by car using the Ancona Sud exit off the main A14 motorway. There are also regular buses from Ancona.

Pergola

This shapely small town, set in the vineyard-dotted valley of the Cesano river, has a surprising wealth of churches and smart *palazzi*, many of which date back to the 13th century.

The church of **San Francesco**, in the medieval quarter of the town, was founded by contemporary disciples in 1255, less than thirty years after St Francis' death. Many of the other churches, including the beautiful octagonal domed **Santa Maria delle Tinte**, date from the 17th and 18th Centuries, when the town was a flourishing centre for craftsmen and artists.

But above all, Pergola is famous for the ***Bronzi Dorati***, extraordinary gilded bronze statues of two equestrian figures and two women, which date back to the 1st century AD (see box).

The town's other attraction is a heavily perfumed, purple wine made with local red *vernaccia* grapes and sold as Vernaccia di Pergola.

The Gilded Bronzes of Pergola

This magnificent group of equestrian sculptures, dating back to the Roman period, was unearthed in a field near Pergola in 1946 and is a rare example of its kind. The life-size statues, made of copper alloy with a large lead content and gilded with gold leaf, weigh around 900 kilograms.

The group comprise two female standing figures and two high ranking cavaliers in military dress on two richly decorated horses.

At the time of their discovery they were in extremely poor condition and badly fragmented. A long process of restoration has brought them back close to their former splendour.

The question of their date and identity has been the subject of considerable debate. The most intriguing theory is that the bronzes were destroyed and buried on the orders of the Emperor Tiberius in the 1st century AD and that they represent his mother Livia, Agrippina, wife of his nephew Germanicus, and her sons Drusus III and Nero, against whom Tiberius had decreed a *damnatio memoriae* and the destruction of all images of the family. According to this theory, the statues were destroyed and taken far from Rome so that they could not be found.

Another theory suggests the statues were made at a nearby Roman foundry, perhaps at Sentinum, some 20 kms south of Pergola, and were of an important Roman family of the 1st century BC. The family may then have fallen into disgrace, perhaps implicated in the murder of Julius Caesar.

Tourist information:

Corso Matteotti
tel: 0721 778434 fax: 0721 778818
www.bronzidorati.com/

Getting there:

Pergola, in Pesaro & Urbino province, lies some 35 kms inland from the coast on the SS424, exit off the main A14 motorway at Marotta.

Pesaro

The capital of the region's northern *Pesaro e Urbino* province, this appealing city is in turn an attractive seaside resort, a thriving fishing port and an important manufacturing centre. Its elegant broad streets have worthwhile sights to hold your attention and after a day on one of its uncrowded beaches, a fish supper by the sea is hard to beat.

At the heart of the city lies the wide main square, **Piazza del Popolo**. Sipping a cool drink from one of the bars flanking the *piazza*, admire the sea-horses and tritons that decorate the sparkling fountain in the centre. Then let your eyes wander over the **Palazzo Ducale** that vies for your attention with the imperious post office building. The clean-lined Renaissance palace, recently restored, was built in the middle of the 15th century by the ruling Sforza family. It now houses local government offices and an exhibition space open to the public. Take a moment to walk into the imposing courtyard.

Rossini & his Festival

Gioachino Rossini was the first of a succession of operatic composers who were to bring Italy to the forefront in world opera. Born in Pesaro in 1792, he began his composing career at the age of 18 and for the next nineteen years composed 36 operas which brought him success and wealth unparalleled among composers of the time.

Among his works are such legendary names as *The Barber of Seville*, *The Thieving Magpie*, and *William Tell*. *Tell* was Rossini's last opera but he was to live for another 39 years, composing little more than two religious works. He moved to France in the early 1820s and remained there until his death in 1868. He is buried at Florence in the church of Santa Croce.

Pesaro remains an important pilgrimage centre for Rossini enthusiasts and is the setting, each August, for the prestigious opera festival dedicated to his work.

www.rossinioperafestival.it

Leaving the square towards the sea along Via Rossini you'll find on your right the modest house where Italy's great opera *bel canto* composer Gioachino Rossini was born in 1792; it is now a small shrine to the composer (see boxed text).

The city was once noted for its ceramic workshops that turned out the brightly glazed earthenware known as *majolica*. In the **Musei Civici** (Civic Museums) in Piazza Toschi Mosca (just off Via Rossini) you can browse through one of Italy's finest collections of renaissance and baroque pottery, much of it striking for its spontaneous, almost modern, use of colour and design.

If crockery leaves you cold, the warmth of **Giovanni Bellini's** masterpiece, the *Coronation of the Virgin* in the adjoining **Pinacoteca** shouldn't. This large painting with a series of smaller panels, originally created as an altarpiece, catches the eye with its sun-drenched colours and rounded, sculptural figures. The gallery also has a large collection of interesting, if less important, Renaissance pictures.

The castle in the background of Bellini's painting is the Sforza family fortress at **Gradara** (page 96); it was Pesaro's ruling lord, Costanzo Sforza, who commissioned the picture from the Venetian artist. If you're driving north on the A 14 motorway you will catch sight of it a few miles from Pesaro - the view has hardly changed since the day Bellini painted it.

Centuries before the Sforza family ruled Pesaro, the city was already a thriving Roman colony, founded in 184 BC, probably on the foundations of an even older settlement. For lost property from Roman *Pisaurum* visit the **Museo Archeologico Oliveriano** in Via Mazza to the west of the main square.

Keep heading straight down Via Rossini and you will eventually find yourself on the sea-front and looking at one of the city's most flamboyant buildings, the **Villino Ruggeri**. This heavily-stuccoed confection is one of the finest examples of the Italian Liberty style that swept the Adriatic Riviera at the turn of the 20th century.

Like most Italian **beaches**, the 3km strand here is laid out with serried ranks of umbrellas and deck chairs but it is rarely overcrowded. For a more secluded beach with green hills as a backdrop, make for **Baia Flaminia** just to the north of the centre. As well as sections with all the gear where you have to pay, there are also free stretches of public beach. You'll also find free, uncluttered public beaches just south of the town on the SS16 road towards Fano.

Tourist information:

via Rossini, 41
tel: 0721 359501 fax: 0721 33930
www.turismo.pesarourbino.it/

Getting there:

Pesaro is on the main Milano-Bari railway line with frequent trains that serve most of the region's coastal towns and beyond. For drivers, the town lies on the A14 Bologna-Pescara toll motorway, exit Pesaro. Regular coach services from outside the railway station and from the coach station in Piazzale Matteotti in the centre (details from the Tourist information office) run to nearby seaside resorts as well as major inland towns, including Urbino.

Piobbico, Apecchio & the Serriola Pass

The SS257 road winds its way from Acqualagna to Città di Castello in Umbria over the **Bocca Serriola**, an atmospheric but not excessively high pass (730 m) over the Apennines, and takes in a pair of small but delightful mountain towns.

First stop is **Piobbico**. Above the small modern nucleus along the main road stands **Castello Brancaleoni** with its *borghetto*, a cluster of crumbling medieval houses clinging like limpets to the hillside around it. Originally built in the 13th century by the ruling Brancaleoni family, the castle was given an elegant Renaissance facelift in the 1570s. After years of neglect, it has now being given a much deserved restoration - it is open to the public between June and September at weekends, but even when closed it's worth walking up to peer into the courtyard. The town is celebrated in Italy for being the home of the *Club dei Brutti*, an association for the world's downtrodden uglies - their motto reads "Ugliness is a virtue; beauty is slavery".

Further on, the small mountain town of **Apecchio** with a strong medieval stamp nestles deep in the Apennines mountains. No single great monument, but lashings of local colour. In the mountains around, charcoal burners still build their fires and the elderly widows that linger in the streets look as if they come from central casting.

Best sights are the hump-back medieval bridge and **Palazzo Ubaldini** which houses a fine fossil museum. Around 4 km NE of Apecchio on the SS257 follow the sign off to Monte Nerone, to snake up to the sublime uplands of this craggy limestone mountain.

Tourist information:
www.comune.piobbico.pu.it/
www.comune.apecchio.ps.it/

Recanati

A remarkably attractive small hill town, Recanati is close to the heart of many Italians as the birthplace of one the country's great poets, Giacomo Leopardi (1798-1837) (see below).

This dignified place, just inland from the Adriatic Sea, is strung out along the crest of a hill. It was renowned in the 16th and 17th century for its commercial fair, one of the most important in the Papal States, and its wide streets and comfortable buildings still have a mercantile bearing.

Nowadays, however, it is remembered for its famous son, Leopardi. He passed a hothouse childhood, self-imprisoned in his father's classics-filled library and spent the rest of his life trying to recapture in his pessimistic verse the illusion of happiness, glimpsed fleetingly as a boy in Recanati. **Palazzo Leopardi** at the southern edge of town, where he was born and brought up, holds memorabilia, manuscripts and the magnificent **library** in which he passed his youth. Around almost every corner of the town, plaques mark spots referred to in his poems.

Recanati was also the birthplace of the great 20th century tenor, Beniamino Gigli and the **Museo Gigli** in the *Palazzo Comunale*, or town hall, on central Piazza Leopardi holds a collection of his costumes from some 30 operas, a mock-up of his dressing-room and some of the many presents he received, including a walking stick that once belonged to Verdi.

Giacomo Leopardi

Leopardi, 19th century Italy's greatest poet, was born in Recanati in 1798. His father, Count Monaldo Leopardi, was an impoverished aristocrat who had withdrawn from the world into the safety of his library, and encouraged his son to follow his example.

By the age of sixteen Giacomo had read all of the great texts in Latin and Greek and knew English, French, Spanish and Hebrew. But the effect of his self-imposed imprisonment upon his health was disastrous - his eyesight began to fail and he developed curvature of the spine which gradually reduced him to an invalid.

By the age of twenty he had formed a thoroughly pessimistic view of life which was to influence his entire literary output. He saw life as tedious and purposeless and regarded any form of optimism for the future as a nonsense. Even technological advance, he thought, would lead to human misery. He saw it as the task of the poet to create the illusion of happiness which we briefly glimpse in childhood before it is snatched away from us forever.

He began his career as a poet in 1820. The heroes in most of his early poetry were patriots striving to overcome adversity. But his greatest poetry dates from the period 1829-1932 and includes *La quieta dopo la tempestà*, *L'infinito*, and *A Silvia*. However, his fame during his lifetime was established by his prose works which included dialogues and essays which he classed as *Operette Morali* (1827) and his *Pensieri* and letters.

By 1833, his health was deteriorating and he and his companion Antonio Ranieri moved to the warmer climate of Naples. He lived and worked there until his death in 1837.

The museum in **Villa Colloredo-Mels**, a splendid 18th century villa on the edge of town, holds Recanati's greatest art treasure, a room with four of **Lorenzo**

Lotto's finest pictures, including a most haunting *Annunciation* packed with almost breathless narrative detail - a high spot in any art-lover's tour of the central Marche.

Other delights in Recanati include the **Cathedral** of San Flaviano with its magnificent 17th century wood ceiling and the **Teatro Persiani**, another of the Marche's unexpectedly grand 19th century theatres.

Tourist information:

Piazza Giacomo Leopardi, 31
tel. e fax: 071 981471
www.comune.recanati.mc.it/

Getting there:

Recanati is a shortish drive along the SS77off the main A14 toll motorway, exit Loreto. There is a regular bus service from Ancona. Nearest railway stations are Loreto & Porto Recanati on the main Milano-Bari line.

San Benedetto del Tronto

Although this is one of the Marche's most popular seaside resorts, it is also a thriving town that doubles as one of the most important fishing ports on Italy's Adriatic coast. And with over 7,000 palm trees on its wide promenade, it has a touch of tropical charm.

In summer this is a popular place, but with 8 kms of wide sandy palm-lined **beach** there is plenty of space for everyone. And although it has a great deal of old-world elegance, it's also a lively place with a fun nightlife that is great for younger visitors.

The most pleasant stretch of **beach** - and the highest concentration of good hotels - runs from the centre of town southwards. The beach to the north of the large port area is less inviting although it offers many more stretches of free, public beach.

The older part of the town sits above the main resort, on the far side of **Corso Mazzini**, with its **castle** and winding, narrow streets of brick houses.

As well as catching fish, its inhabitants also take the eating of them seriously and there are plenty of moderately priced restaurants to satisfy their demanding tastes. This is the place to try the Marche version of fish stew - **brodetto** - which traditionalists claim should be made with 13 species of fish, no more, no less..

> **Il brodetto Sambenedettese**
>
> Each of the main towns on the Marche coast has its own authentic recipe for *brodetto*, or Marche fish stew. But San Benedetto's is claimed to be the best. It is probably better to try it in the town, but if you can't, here is the recipe.
>
> In a pan lightly brown some onion in olive oil with a small piece of hot chilli. Then add tomato puree, a cup of fish stock and chopped octopus and squid and leave them on a low flame until the fish is tender. Meanwhile in another large pan lay the following fish in layers starting with mantis prawn (which is similar to scampi), and alternating with a layer of the cooked tomato and squid. The other fish needed are goby, monkfish, mullet, *cefali* (a rather beastly looking white fish) and John Dory. The final layer should be mussels and another mollusc known locally as *moscioli*. Bathe the lot with a little white wine and gently cook covered. Serve the stew on pieces of toasted bread. Use fish heads from three other species for the stock and you arrive at the magical 13 species.

Tourist information:

via delle Tamerici, 5
tel: 0735 595088 fax: 0735 576190
http://www.larivieradellepalme.it/home/index.cfm

Getting there:

San Benedetto del Tronto is on the main Milano-Bari railway line with frequent trains that serve most of the region's coastal towns and beyond. For drivers, the town lies off the A14 Bologna-Pescara toll motorway, exit San Benedetto del Tronto.

Sant'Angelo in Vado

This small agricultural and commercial centre in mountain country has an attractive *centro storico* surprisingly rich in fine buildings and good pictures, as well as remarkable Roman mosaics. It was the birthplace of a number of important baroque artists and architects - including the brothers Taddeo and Federico Zuccari who made a name for themselves in Rome in the second half of the 16th centruy - and is well worth exploring.

The town was once the Roman *Tiphernum Metaurense* and when rebuilt after the wars between the Byzantines and Ostrogoths was dedicated to the Archangel Michael, hence its name Sant'Angelo.

Look out for the 13th century **Palazzo della Ragione** with its splendid bell-tower and **Palazzo Fagnani** which houses the town hall and a large *Sacra Conversazione* by Federico Zuccari.

Of the many admirable churches the **Duomo**, with a painting by Gentile da Fabriano, and the church of **San Francesco** stand out.

One of the most remarkable sights in the town is the **Domus del Mito**, or House of the Myth, the remains of a 1st century AD Roman villa with some 1,000 square metres of elaborate, polychrome mosaics. Only recently discovered, they represent one of the finest ancient Roman discoveries in central Italy in recent years.

During the last weekends of October the town hosts the *Mostra Nazionale del Tartufo Bianco Pregiato*, an excellent chance to taste white truffles and see the town at its best.

Rearing Truffles

The town is also known for its contribution to gastronomy; the first nursery in Italy to successfully cultivate commercially the much-prized truffle is here; saplings of selected trees have their roots impregnated with the spores of the underground fungus, and are then planted in areas with the very particular soil necessary. After a wait of some ten years and much luck, the first truffles are ready to be dug up by truffle hunters and their sniffer dogs. The technique has proved so successful that large tracts of the *umbro-marchigiani* Apennines are being turned over to truffle reserves.

Tourist information:

tel: 0722 88455
www.domusdelmito.com/
www.mostratartufo.it/

Getting there:

Sant'Angelo in Vado, in Pesaro e Urbino province, is about 25 kms west of Urbino on the SS73 Bocca Trabaria pass road.

Sarnano

The attractive spa town of Sarnano lies roughly half way between the two provincial capitals of Macerata and Ascoli Piceno. Its waters are claimed to be beneficial for a whole gamut of complaints, including gout, arthritis and liver problems.

The modern town is overlooked by its quiet, rather austere, medieval *borgo*, topped by two solid towers, which has been left very much alone by the modern-day development. A steep, winding street leads up to a beguiling little square, **Piazza Alta**, flanked by the church of Santa Maria Assunta and the town's medieval municipal buildings - Palazzo del Popolo with its finely decorated gothic-romanesque portal, the Torre Civica, the Palazzo dei Priori and the Palazzetto del Podestà.

The more recent Palazzo Municipale, half way down in via Leopardi, houses a small **art gallery** which includes a *Madonna and Child with two angels* by Vittore Crivelli, brother of the more famous Carlo.

The town has several hotels which provide a convenient base camp for exploring the Sibillini Mountains, and a number of inviting restaurants. A good wide road winds up from Piazza della Libertà, in the modern part of the town, through beech coppices and limestone crags until, after about twelve kilometres, it reaches **Sasso Tetto**, one of the Marche's small ski resorts, and well equipped with ski lifts and accommodation.

Bath Time

Italians still flock to health-giving mineral springs as they have done since Roman times and a number of spa towns in the Marche have seen a revival in recent years. The ten *terme* in the region are, from north to south: Monte Grimano, Carignano, Macerata Feltria, Petriano, Aspio, San Vittore delle Chiuse, Tolentino, Torre di Palme, Sarnano and Acquasanta.

Each of them tends to specialize in the treatment of specific complaints depending on the nature of their waters although many now promote themselves as a good excuse to relax and be pampered.

Tourist information:

Largo Ricciardi, 1
tel: 0733 657144 fax: 0733 657343
ww.montiazzurriturismo.it/

Getting there

Sarnano, in Macerata province, lies some 30 kms south of Macerata on the main SS78 road.

Senigallia

The locals call it the "spiaggia di velluto", or velvet beach, and Senigallia certainly boasts one of the finest strands in the Marche – some 12 kms of fine sand. But this historic old town also makes an interesting base for touring the central Marche's attractive inland hill towns if you don't want to spend all your time by the sea.

Although its prosperity nowadays depends much on tourism, it is a town with a long history. Its name bears witness to its earliest inhabitants - the *Galli Senoni*, a

Celtic tribe who settled here around the 4th century BC. In the 15th century is was widely celebrated for its enormous commercial fair - the Maddalena Fair.

Still today its *centro storico*, or old centre, has a certain solid mercantile grandeur, particularly in the tall old blocks that line the canal. While wandering through the lanes of the centre also notice the low, thick-walled style of many of the buildings - specially designed in centuries past to avoid earthquake damage.

The finest monument is the old fort, the **Rocca Roveresca**, built in 1480 by the ruling Della Rovere family. In the summer its courtyard echoes to the sound of classical music concerts. On the beach stands the handsome ***Rotonda a Mare***, a rare example of an Italian seaside pier, dating back to 1933.

Senigallia's other great pride is the number of good restaurants where you can, naturally, eat the best of the Adriatic catch; the town has two restaurants – **Uliassi** and the **Madonnina del Pescatore** - that regulalry feature in lists of Italy's top ten restaurants.

Tourist information:

Piazzale Morandi, 2
tel: 071 7922725 fax: 071 7924930
www.comune.senigallia.an.it/

Getting there:

Senigallia is on the main Milano-Bari railway line with frequent trains that serve most of the region's coastal towns and beyond. For drivers, the town lies on the A14 Bologna-Pescara toll motorway, exit Senigallia.

Serra San Quirico

This small medieval village is a good example of the region's small-scale gems that are always worth a detour, preferably around lunchtime for some *cucina tipica* in one of two excellent local restaurants.

Turn off in the uninspiring modern village on the main road to climb up to the old *centro storico*. The first thing you'll notice as the village comes into view are the *copertelle*, or covered walkways built above the 12th century walls. You can stroll through them taking in the splendid views of the valley below.

Then search out the **Church of Santa Lucia**, one of the region's prettiest late baroque churches built in 1650 on an older church. In amongst the gilt and the cherubs are magnificent paintings by Guido Reni, Pasqualino Rossi, and the Cavaliere D'Arpino.

Next door the town's Map Museum (*Cartoteca Storica Regionale*) holds a collection of regional maps dating back to the 1200s.

When you have finished, take a coffee in the small opera-set **piazza** with a pretty fountain and a flag-draped town hall.

Another good reason to visit here is to try the town's *calcioni* pastries with their curious sweet and sour cheese and lemon filling.

Getting there:

Serra San Quirico in Ancona province is 20 kms SW of Jesi and 25 kms NE of Fabriano.

Sibillini Mountains

Wherever you find yourself in the Marche, the Apennine mountains are never far away. They form the region's western border and offer some of its finest scenery as well as providing a home for some of Italy's most fascinating wildlife. And perhaps no part of the mountains is as impressive as the southern Marche's **Monti Sibillini**, a large part of which is now a natural park (see below).

The great limestone massif of the Sibillini Mountains includes one of the highest peaks on the Italian mainland - **Monte Vettore** at 2,476 mts - and the wild tarns and windswept high plains of the Sibillini provide some of the region's most spectacular landscapes.

But hiking or even driving up here is not for the faint-hearted. Roads are slow, tracks not always clearly marked and the weather can easily become poor.

The itinerary on page **67** will bring you close up to the mountains and includes a detour into their heart to see some of the most memorable spots. Remember to fill up with petrol before heading off the beaten track.

Chiselled by glaciers and limestone erosion, these mountains possess some outstanding natural sights. These include the high tarn, **Lago di Pilato** (a somewhat dubious tradition has it that Pontius Pilate is buried here), and the awesome **Infernaccio Gorge**. Other delights include the great **upland plains** which are a mass of flowers in spring.

The most impressive of these other-worldly places is just over the border in Umbria and is known as the **Piano Grande**. It lies below the village of Castelluccio and is famous across Italy for its lentils. In May and June, this huge expanse of treeless plateau, 1,250 metres above sea level, eight kilometres long and five wide, is transformed with a carpet of wild flowers.

Monti Sibillini Natural Park

The **Parco Naturale dei Monti Sibillini**, in the south-west part of the massif, is the region's largest nature park, spreading over 40 kms of mountain peaks and continuing westwards into Umbria. The mountains take their name from a legend that one of the sibyls hid here in a cave on Monte Sibilla known as *Grotta della Sibilla* when she was chased out of the Underworld.

Monte Vettore (2,476 mts), at the centre of the park, is the highest mountain in the Region. The huge rocky walls and crags in its eastern side, with such eerie names as Pizzo del Diavolo (Devil's beard) and Gola dell'Infernaccio (Hell's Gorge), are almost as dramatic as the landscape of the Dolomites.

The area is a botanist's paradise. Alpine edelweiss (*Leontopodion nivale*), martagon lily, bear berry, Apennine cinquefoil and alpine buckthorn are just some of the species here. The park is also rich in bird life - buzzards, kestrels, sparrow hawks as well as rare sightings of golden eagle, peregrine falcon, rock partridge, eagle owl and chough.

Tourist information:

Piazza del Forno,
62039 - Visso (MC)
tel: 0737 972711 fax: 0737 972707
www.sibillini.net/

Tolentino

Tolentino in the heartland of the southern-central Marche is a thriving medieval town set in rolling hills. Pilgrims come from across Italy to visit the shrine of **St Nicholas of Tolentino** (1245-1305). A multitude of miracles have been attributed to this Augustinian friar who passed the last thirty years of his life here.

Even if you don't have any favours to ask of him, visit the handsome **Basilica** where he is buried to marvel at the grandiose 14th century Giottoesque **frescoes** in the gothic **Cappellone di San Nicola**. These vivid frescoes painted in the early years of the 1300s by Pietro da Rimini, are some of perhaps the most beautiful in the whole of the Marche. Spare time also to linger in the tranquil romanesque cloister alongside the church.

History was made in 1797 at **Palazzo Parisani-Bezzi** in Via della Pace when **Napoleon**, in the wake of his successful invasion of the Papal States, forced Pope Pius VI to sign the Peace of Tolentino.

If you enjoy riddles, make for the splendid central **Piazza della Libertà** to figure out the multiple clock faces on one of the Marche's oddest medieval clock towers, including one for the phases of the moon.

Tolentino also boasts "The International Museum of Caricature and Humour in Art" in its new home, **Palazzo Sangallo**. Here you can see some 13,000 comic works by artists from across the world.

There are plenty of other interesting corners to explore in this lively town with no shortage of places for good, simple *marchigiani* food.

> **St Nicholas of Tolentino**
>
> A *marchigiano* saint through and through, San Nicola da Tolentino was born near Fermo around 1245. He became a friar in the Order of St Augustine and in 1275 entered the monastery at Tolentino where he died in 1305.
>
> Although a noted preacher and pastoral worker, his fame rests on the numerous miracles attributed to his intercession.
>
> His remains now rest in the dimly-lit crypt of the Basilica.

Tourist information:

Piazza della Libertà
tel: 0733 972937
www.vivitolentino.it/
www.sannicoladatolentino.it/

Getting there:

Tolentino, in Macerata province, lies well inland in the southern-central Marche off the SS77. If you are coming from the main A14 toll motorway, take the Macerata exit. The town is on the Fabriano branch rail line which connects with the main Milano-Bari line at Civitanova Marche.

Urbania

Attractively sited on the fast-flowing Metauro river, this striking small town is surprisingly rich in impressive buildings and works of art. Formerly known as Castel Durante, it was renamed in honour of Pope Urban VIII in 1636, shortly after the last Duke of Urbino handed over his lands to the Papal States.

The imposing **Palazzo Ducale** was originally a 13th century feudal stronghold later smartened up by Duke Federico of Urbino - his favourite architect, Francesco di Giorgio Martini, was responsible for a large part of the facelift.

Cross the gracious courtyard to see an appealing **museum** of paintings, ancient maps and globes, and Renaissance **ceramics** (16th century Castel Durante boasted 32 *majolica*, or painted pottery workshops and was one of the most important centres for ceramics in Italy).

Other monuments to note while strolling in the shade of the **arcaded streets** include the **Bramante Theatre** (Urbania is one of two cities claiming the great Renaissance architect as its son) and the church of **Santa Chiara**. The last Duke of Urbino, Francesco Maria II Della Rovere is buried in the **Chiesa del Crocifisso**; like many other buildings in Urbania this church was badly damaged by Allied bombing in 1944.

You will find the town's strangest offering behind the altar of the **Chiesetta dei Morti** in Via Ugolini - the *Cimitero delle Mummie*. Here a dozen leathery mummified corpses hang like washing in a row of glass-fronted cabinets. They were put on display in 1813 after they were discovered in the ground below, preserved by a rare type of mould. The custodian takes great delight in opening the cupboards to show you the body with stab wounds and the pregnant woman with a mummified foetus.

If you arrive from Sant'Angelo in Vado look out for the striking Renaissance **villa**, the *Barco Ducale*, just before the town - it was once a hunting lodge for the Dukes of Urbino.

Tourist information:

Corso Vittorio Emanuele, 21
tel: 0722 313140 fax: 0722 313179
www.urbania-casteldurante.it/

Getting there:

Urbania lies less than 20 km west of Urbino on the SS73bis.

Know Your Onions

One of the region's more curious folk traditions is the use of onions at Urbania to foretell the coming year's weather. On the night of 24 January twelve onion sections - one for each month - are sprinkled with salt and left outside; in the morning the way the salt has dissolved is examined and the weather forecast made.

The secret of reading the onions of Urbania is said to date back to medieval times and is currently guarded by *Signora* Emanuela Forlini, a local teacher who inherited the skill from her father and grandfather.

Urbino

Urbino remains one of the most important towns in the Marche for the tourist in search of great Italian art and architecture and its narrow streets well reward the curious traveller. Its *centro storico* boasts the honour of being included in the UNESCO list of World Heritage Sites.

During the second half of the 15th century, Urbino's windy hill was the home of one of the most illustrious courts in Europe. Duke Federico da Montefeltro gathered around him the greatest painters, poets and scholars of his day in one of Italy's most beautiful Renaissance palaces, a palace that still stands as an eloquent and fitting memorial to this quintessential Renaissance man.

For the best first impression, approach the town from the west to see the soaring twin towers of the palace that give Urbino its unmistakable skyline; already you will see that it was built by a benevolent - at least for those violent times - and secure ruler who had no need to intimidate or brag.

The hub of the town is the animated triangle of **Piazza della Repubblica** that lies in a dip between the twin hills on which the town stands. From here follow the signs up to the **Palazzo Ducale**. The opening times are 9am to 7pm Tuesday-Sunday, and 9am to 2pm Monday.

The Palace entrance might appear simpler than you would expect – it was designed to welcome more than impress. The inner courtyard is a masterly example of early Renaissance architecture, a masterpiece of proportion and light carried out with the deftest of touches. Remember this was the first of its kind, similar courtyards you will see across Italy are mere copies.

None of the rooms of the palace were designed to oppress with grandeur but were built on a human scale and decorated with sobriety. Nowadays they house the **Galleria Nazionale delle Marche** - a remarkable collection of paintings including one of the world's greatest and most enigmatic images, Piero della Francesca's **Flagellation of Christ**.

Other great pictures here are Piero della Francesca's **Madonna di Senigallia** that could almost be an interior painting by Vermeer, Raphael's **La Muta**, the Silent One, a portrait of an anonymous gentlewoman who seems as if she would talk to us if she wanted to, and a famous vision of the **Ideal City** by an unknown hand (possibly Piero della Francesca's) and now much used by art designers to illustrate books on the Renaissance.

The Duke's **Studiolo** is the most remarkable room in the palace. His tiny study was entirely decorated in exquisite trompe l'oeil inlaid woodwork panels, some based on designs by Botticelli.

To understand the complex domestic organisation that propped up what the poet W.B.Yeats described as "That grammar school of courtesies/Where wit and beauty learned their trade/Upon Urbino's windy hill" in his poem *To a Wealthy Man*, visit the warren of cellars, kitchens, laundry rooms, stables and even an ice store in the *Sotterranei*, or basements.

No single architect can be credited as the creative genius behind this blueprint for the unfortified Renaissance dwelling, although Luciano Laurana and Francesco di Giorgio Martini figure large. It has to be seen rather as the sum total of Duke Federico's enlightened patronage.

Few traces remain of earlier Roman *Urbinum Metaurense* - see some in the exhaustive collection of ancient stone inscriptions in the **Museo Archeologico** on the ground floor of the Ducal Palace - and virtually the entire city within the walls dates from the 15th and 16th century; the ghost of Federico would still not lose his way in the maze of pink-bricked alleys.

In Piazza Rinascimento, the square outside the palace, note the **Egyptian obelisk**. Originally raised in Egypt in 580 BC, looted by the Romans in AD 90 and given to Urbino in 1737, it is one of only a couple of obelisks you'll find in Italy outside Rome.

Giovanni Santi was a court painter at Urbino who might have been consigned to the lumber room of art history if he hadn't been the father of the divine **Raphael**. Few can doubt that Raphael's childhood at the court helped mould his genius. The house where he was born is now a delightful little **museum** - a simple fresco of the **Madonna and Child** in one of the rooms may have been one of his earliest works. You will find it in Via Raffaello which runs up from Piazza della Repubblica.

Federico da Montefeltro

The most famous member of the Montefeltro line was born in 1422 to a small-time noble family that ruled over an insignificant square of the Italian chess-board. Yet within sixty years he had become "the light of Italy" and the paradigm of Renaissance man, as skilled in letters as in arms.

His portrait, together with his young son, Guidobaldo, by the Spanish painter Pedro Berruguete in Urbino's Ducal Palace neatly portrays this duality of scholar and warrior - studiously reading a weighty manuscript, he keeps his helmet by his side. As in nearly all portraits of the Duke, including Piero della Francesca's famous painting in the Uffizi, we only see his left profile; a swordblow in a tournament earlier in his life had cost him his right eye; he had surgeons lower the bridge of his nose to increase his field of vision in his one remaining eye, hence the distinctive beaked profile.

He made his money as one of the most successful *condottiere*, or hired generals, of his time. Always fighting on short-term contracts and strictly for cash on the nail, he displayed the timeless Italian talent of never taking sides - he managed once to fight for Florence against the Pope only to later take up the Papal banner against the Florentines.

His fortune made, he turned to the arts as enthusiastically as he had to war and settled down to create his sparkling court. Almost all the great names of the *Quattrocento* passed through his palace, and his library was reckoned amongst the largest in Europe.

On his death in 1482, his sickly son, Guidobaldo, managed to keep alive the splendour of the court with the help of his emancipated wife Elisabetta Gonzaga. Baldesar Castiglione wrote his famous *Book of the Courtier*, the classic account of the Renaissance ideal, while a member of Guidobaldo's retinue.

On his death in 1508, the Dukedom passed to the Della Rovere family and Urbino's decline began. The light was finally extinguished in 1631 when the last Duke, Francesco Maria II Della Rovere, died and the Duchy passed to the Papal States - its palace stripped of its treasures, Urbino sank into unbroken torpor.

Hike on up to the summit of the steep hill to find a striking statue of the painter and grandstand **views** of the countryside around Urbino.

Hunt out the **Oratorio di San Giovanni Battista** in Via Barocci to see a small church entirely decorated in 1416 with wall-to-ceiling **frescoes** by the *marchigiani* painters Jacopo and Lorenzo Salimbeni. Ignore the fact that few outside the Marche have ever heard of the brothers; use your own eyes and enjoy the brilliance of their earthy vision of the life of St John the Baptist and a terrifying Crucifixion - or just count the number of playful small dogs you can spot in the lively scenes. Next door is a glorious 16th century plasterwork *presepio*, or crib, by Federico Brandani in the **Oratorio di San Giuseppe**.

A rarely visited but nevertheless delightful stop is the ***Orto Botanico***. This small, walled botanical garden is full of rare plants, the shade is welcome, and there are definitely no paintings. The entrance is in Via Bramante.

As you leave Urbino pause to pay your last respects at the **tombs** of Duke Federico and his son, Guidobaldo, in the fine church of **San Bernardino**. It was built in 1491 by Francesco di Giorgio Martini and stands on the hill above the junction for the Pesaro road - follow the signs.

Tourist information:

Piazza Rinascimento, 1
tel: 0722 2613 fax: 0722 2441
www.comune.urbino.ps.it/

Getting there:

Urbino lies some 35 kms inland from Pesaro on the SS423; if you're coming from the A14 toll motorway, exit at Pesaro. Park below the city walls below the twin towers of the Ducal Palace in Piazza del Mercatale where there is a large undergorund car park.. A good coach service runs regularly from/to Pesaro station on the Milano-Bari rail line.

Visso

The small but elegant town of **Visso** in the Monti Sibillini National Park holds one of the architectural delights of the southern Marche. It's also a good base if you want to visit the staggeringly beautiful high plateau of the **Piano Grande**.

Driving through Porta Santa Maria, we enter **Piazza Capuzi**, an intimate triangular square of medieval stuccoed buildings, with both rounded and pointed gothic arches and stone corbels, presided over by the **Palazzo dei Governatori**. Across the way, to the left, in the adjoining **Piazza dei Martiri Vissani** is the splendid romanesque-gothic collegiate **church of Santa Maria**, its beautiful main portal flanked by two carved lions.

Inside the church, you'll find a gigantic 14th century fresco of Saint Christopher with an almost pagan stare to it, which looms up nearly to touch the coffered ceiling. Admire also the romanesque baptistery in the rear corner of the nave with a pair of magnificent 14th century carved stone sarcophagi.

In the same delightful square stands the ex-church of **Sant'Agostino**, now an attractively laid out museum with a collection of original manuscripts by **Giacomo Leopardi**, including one of only two manuscripts of his most famous poem *L'Infinito*.

Several shops in the atmospheric **centro storico** sell cured meats for which this area is famous. These include the soft pork salami, *ciauscolo*, , and *coglioni di asino* (donkey meat and called *coglioni*, or testicles, only because of the shape).

Some 10 kms outside the town, off the road for Camerino, stands the **Sanctuary of Macereto**, a perfectly symetrical jewel of a Renaissance church built 1,000 metres up on a high plateau in 1529 to house a miraculous statue of the Madonna. An atmospheric sight in the wilderness and well worth the detour. Inside are outstanding frescoes (1580-82) by Simone de Magistris.

Tourist information:

Piazza M. Vissani
tel: 0737 9239 (summer only)
www.sibillini.net/

Getting there:

Visso, in Macerata province, is on the western edge of the Sibillini Mountains and is best reached on the SS209 from Camerino or Tolentino.

Useful Information

Getting to the Marche

By air: The low fares airline RyanAir flies from London Stansted to the region's own airport, Ancona Falconara. Flight time is under two hours and the airport is a half-hour's bus ride from Ancona city centre and mainline rail station. There are also flights from Ancona to other destinations including Rome and Munich. Ancona airport website: www.aeroportomarche.com/

RyanAir also fly to Rimini airport just over the Marche's northern border and Perugia in neighbouring Umbria.

Many airlines, including Alitalia and British Airways, have regular flights to Bologna airport (around three hours by car from Ancona). Rome airport (three hours by car to Ancona) also offers a wide choice of airlines.

By rail: The larger towns on the coastal Milano-Bari main rail line are served by direct international services in summer to Munich and Vienna. Other European destinations are also served via easy changes at Milano or Bologna.

By car: The Marche is two days journey away from Britain. The cost of motorway tolls, petrol, meals, and overnight accommodation soon eats into any savings you might hope to make by bringing your own car, though it gives you the freedom to stash away a case or two of wine and olive oil to take back and may be cheaper than hiring a car here if you're staying for more than a couple of weeks.

Ferries from/to Ancona: Ancona is one of the most important ports on the Adriatic for regular, all-year car and passenger ferries to Greece, Croatia, Montenegro, Albania and Turkey. The main ferry companies include Anek Lines, Minoan Lines and Strintzis Lines. For more information consult www.doricaportservices.it/.

Getting around in the Marche

By rail: The Ferrovie dello Stato (FS), the Italian State Railways has two main lines in the Marche. The coastal Milano-Bari line links up most of the seaside resorts while the cross-Italy Ancona-Rome line provides a useful link with the towns of Jesi and Fabriano. Other branch lines head inland from Civitanova Marche to Macerata (continuing on to Fabriano) and from San Benedetto del Tronto to Ascoli Piceno in the south. For train times visit http://www.trenitalia.com/

By car: Unless you intend to stay put in one of the towns, a car is the easiest way of discovering the Marche. See *Driving in the Marche* on facing page.

Taxis: Metered taxis are available in most larger towns - you'll usually find them in ranks by the station or in the main square. Fares, which are always displayed, vary according to location, and like taxis across Europe are not cheap. For long journeys in country areas agree the price beforehand.

By bus: All of the major towns and cities are linked by bus services, run by a number of local bus companies, though services tend to coincide with school hours, stop relatively early in the evening, and rarely run on Sundays. Timetables and routes are available from tourist information offices or local town halls.

Driving in the Marche

Drivers need a current licence and if it is not the current EU type it should be accompanied by a translation in Italian, available from Italian State Tourist offices or the frontier offices of the Italian Automobile Club (A.C.I).

If travelling in your own car you need the vehicle registration book - if it is not in your own name you should also have the owner's written permission to drive the car. You will also need your insurance certificate with a policy extension (in the UK known as a "green card") to make the cover comprehensive while motoring abroad. Without this your insurance is only the legal minimum. The international green card comes with a standard accident report form which must be filled in if you have an accident.

Motorists must have all their documents with them while driving and police spot-checks are common.

The only toll motorway (*autostrada*) in the Marche is the Bologna-Pescara A14 along the Adriatic coast. Some of the main SS (*strada statale*) routes are fast, toll-free dual-carriageways, or *superstrade*. Travelling east-west you are going against the grain of central Italy and will have to put up with slower roads over the Apennines.

But the real point of a car is to leave the crowded highways to meander along the region's relatively empty inland country roads. A few of the smallest roads are unmetalled gravel "white roads". Although they are usually well kept, beware of potholes if your car has a low wheelbase.

The area's antique towns were never built for cars and you will find that some historic centres are now closed to unauthorised traffic. Parking, particularly in the morning and early evening, is often a headache. Where signs indicate a time limit you will have to set a *disco orario* to show your time of arrival - you can buy the disc from most newsagents and garages. If parking spaces are marked with a blue line, it means you have to pay - usually by buying a ticket from a nearby machine.

Off the motorway, many petrol stations close for up to three hours at lunch-time and all day Sunday. Carry a few uncrumpled bank notes to use in the 24-hour, self-service petrol dispensers now common in garage forecourts. Both LPG (*GPL* in Italian) and methane (*metano*) are widely available.

Traffic rules follow European norms and signing follows international conventions. At road junctions, if in doubt, give way to traffic coming from the right. Wearing seat belts both front and back is compulsory and you must carry a reflective warning triangle to be placed at least 50 metres behind your car if you break down. Speed limits are 50 kph in built-up areas, 90 kph on country roads,

110 kph on dual-carriageways and 130 kph on motorways. It is now also compulsory to switch on your dipped headlights during daylight hours on all main roads, and to wear a reflective vest if you break down on a main road and need to leave the car.

Police speed checks are frequent and on-the-spot fines are severe. Contrary to received opinion, the standard of driving in the Marche is generally good and you shouldn't return home prematurely aged.

Away from the big cities, your car is unlikely to be stolen. Luggage, car radios and satellite navigators, however, are an easy target - if you can't take them with you, make sure windows are closed and doors locked.

If your car breaks down, dial ACI (the Italian Automobile Club) on 116 for foreign-language assistance. On motorways there are SOS telephones at regular intervals with two buttons: one for medical assistance and one for breakdowns.

Accommodation notes

Hotels: Most hotels in the Marche are family run and friendly, and only sometimes have English speaking receptionists. As in the rest of Europe, they are graded by stars. One and two star hotels (**) are basic and cheap. Three star hotels (***) are good all-rounders but without expensive frills. Prices vary dramatically depending on location and season. Four star establishments (****) have every comfort you would expect at a higher price.

A full list of hotels is available from the Marche Region Tourism Department, Via Gentile da Fabriano 9, 60125 Ancona (tel: +39 071 8062284; fax: +39 071 8062154 ; email. servizio.turismo@regione.marche.it.) or can be consulted online at www.turismo.marche.it.

On the Farm: The Marche stands in the forefront of *agriturismo*, the scheme which encourages farmers to convert rural buildings into tourist accommodation. These come in the form of self-catering apartments or rural guest house accommodation, often in some of splendid settings and at usually lower prices than many hotels.

Consult the web using "agriturismo" and "Marche" as search terms.

Villa Rental: Another possibility might be to rent a villa or apartment by searching on the web. This is an excellent option if you're looking for a chance to wind down in rural peace. Tripadvisor.com now has good vacation rental listings and Slow Travel at www.slowtrav.com has reliable reviews of rental properties by users.

Renting a Room: If you are touring by car, look out for "bed & breakfast" or "*affittacamera*" signs, These are usually rooms let by private homeowners and tend to be booked in advance during the summer months.

Camping: Down by the coast, campsites abound. They are usually well equipped with shops, shady trees and beach-front locations. They are usually open from late April through to the end of September and charge higher prices in August.

Inland campsites are thinner on the ground. But prices are lower and it's a good way to meet holiday-making Italian families. Many towns are also setting aside areas where motorised camper vans may park for the night.

A full list of camping sites is available from the Marche Region Tourism Department, Via Gentile da Fabriano 9, 60125 Ancona (tel: +39 071 8062284 ; fax: +39 071 8062154 ; email. servizio.turismo@regione.marche.it.) or can be consulted online at www.turismo.marche.it.

National holidays

January 1st and 6th; Easter Monday; April 25th (Liberation Day); May 1st; June 2nd (Republic Day); August 15th (Ferragosto); November 1st; December 8th (Feast of Immaculate Conception), 25th and 26th. Towns also close down on the feast day of their patron saint. The fortnight around August 15th is the peak summer holiday period for Italians, when everyone leaves the cities to flock to the beach.

Language

The *marchigiani* possess the best of northern and south Italy - you will rarely meet extravagant displays of Neapolitan emotion nor the cool indifference of Milan. Try speaking a few words of Italian and your welcome will be that much warmer. If you can only master one line, at least try asking in *Italian* if people speak your language - *Parla inglese?* Remember that outside the main tourist spots, you will not necessarily find people who can speak English. French is a common second language and German is catching on. In the end, however, enthusiastic gestures and smiles will usually get the message through. For a wordlist to help with food shopping see pages 16-17, and for an Italian-English menu translator see page 137.

Weather

Down by the coast summers are hot and winters cool, though somewhat milder as you head south of Ancona, as testifed by the palm trees at San Benedetto del Tronto. Up in the inland mountains expect slightly cooler summers but chilly winters with a distinct possibilty of snow.

The wettest seasons are mid-February to early April and November to mid-December when days of grey mist and rain can set in. In late summer brief but dramatic thunderstorms are common inland.

Ancona	winter	spring	summer	autumn
Average maximum temperature	9.9° C.	17.4° C.	27.3° C.	18.5° C.
Average minimum temperature	1.9° C.	7° C.	16.2° C.	8.7° C.

table of average seasonal temperatures at Ancona Falconara

Clothing

Travel light, even in your own car. Formal clothes are unnecessary unless you are staying in the grander hotels. A smarter outfit, however, for the evening stroll and dinner will help you feel less like a tourist. Many visitors who would never dream of visiting their own churches back home in shorts and halter top get huffy when frowned upon for doing so in Italy - respect convention and cover up bare flesh when visiting religious places.

While lightweight clothing is essential in high summer, you'll need a good sweater or jersey and a raincoat in the spring and autumn. In winter expect cold weather and dress up warmly.

Travel documents

Citizens of the non-Schengen Treaty EU countries, the USA, and numerous other countries only require a valid passport for visits not exceeding three months. If in any doubt, consult your travel agent or your nearest Italian consulate.

Tipping

Tipping is much less expected in the Marche than in Italy's larger tourist destinations. Locals hardly ever tip in restaurants or bars, at most maybe leaving some small change at smarter bars in larger towns. Again people who open up churches or other buildings for you are doing it out of pride in their home town and rarely expect money. Taxi drivers, as anywhere else, expect a tip.

Medical matters

In the event of serious illness or injury, head for the 24-hour first aid, *pronto soccorso*, at any hospital. Pharmacies (*farmacista*) keep normal shop hours and can be spotted by a green cross outside; they operate an emergency 24-hour service on a rotating shift basis, details of which are displayed in the window. Dental treatment is of a high standard but can be costly.

EU residents should carry a European Health Insurance Card (EHIC) entitling them to reciprocal health care in other EU states. Other nationals are strongly advised to get medical and travel insurance before they leave.

For minor aches and pains make straight for the *farmacia* where you can generally get good over-the-counter help.

Money

The currency of Italy is the Euro with one Euro divided into 100 *centesimi*. Banknotes commonly come in denominations of 5, 10, 20, 50, and 100. The higher denomination notes for 200 and 500 are rare, difficult to change and best avoided to reduce the risk of finding yourself with forged currency. Travellers' cheques in major foreign currencies are now less commonly used but generally acceptable. Read the instructions in the event of loss or theft that come with the cheques. The major international credit cards, such as Visa, can be used to get cash in the automatic cash dispensers outside all banks across the Marche - don't forget your PIN code.

The most popular bank in the Marche is - surprise, surprise - the *Banca delle Marche* which has branches in even the most outlandish corners of the region. Banks open Monday to Friday 8.30-13.30 and one hour in the afternoon sometime between 14.30 and 16.00, varying between one bank and another.

Credit cards in place of cash transactions are now almsot as widespread in Italy as in northern Europe. All but the humbler guest-houses and simpler restaurants in central Italy now accept them as do all petrol stations. The most common card sign in central Italy is Carta Si, which includes Visa, Mastercard and Eurocard.

Internet, telephones & postal services

Over half the Italian population now use the internet, but it is still viewed with a degree of diffidence by public authorities and, consequently, some web sites are poorly developed and maintained. Wireless access is also still patchy but slowly catching up with the rest of Europe. Broadband access is good but public internet points are rare.

Italians are some of the world's heaviest users of mobile phones – there are, apparently 50% more mobile phones than people in Italy - and you will rarely have a problem getting a signal. A local pre-paid SIM card (*scheda SIM*) is easily obtainable to use in your own phone. The main mobile operators in Italy are TIM, Vodafone, Wind and 3 Italia.

Pay phones are rarer these days, but can still be found on a few main streets and in some bars; they usually only take a *carta telefonica*, phone cards available in units of €5 from post offices, tobacconists and many bars (you have to break off the top left-hand corner before using it). In a few larger towns Telecom Italia has offices where you can take a cabin and pay for your call afterwards.

Note that *all* Italian telephone numbers must now be dialled with the full area code *even for local calls*. If calling from abroad the initial "0" of the area code is **not** omitted.

To make international direct-dial calls from Italy use 00 + your country code (for Britain 0044, for USA 001 in both cases dropping the initial "0" of the area code). For directory enquiries within Italy dial 12. For information on international calls, dial 176; to make operator-assisted international calls dial 170.

Post offices are open weekdays and Saturday from 8 am to 1.30 pm. Offices in larger towns stay open until 7 pm. If you just want stamps, get them from a tobacconist where you see the large "T" sign.

Post offices will hold letters addressed to individuals on the move until collected in person. The envelope should carry the name of the recipient, the words *Fermo Posta* and the name and post code of the locality. The recipient pays a fee and must show identification to collect the letter.

Information resources

On the Internet:

Marche Voyager – created and run by the author - is the most comprehensive English-language online travel guide to the region, at www.le-marche.com.

Other sites include:

Italian State Tourist Board - www.italia.it

Regional tourism site with accommodation database - www.turismo.marche.it

Ancona Airport - www.airport-ancona.com

Ryanair - www.ryanair.com

Italian State Railways (FS) - www.trenitalia.com

Marche weather (in Italian but easy-to-follow pictures)   meteo.regione.marche.it/

Maps:

The best maps of the area for motorists and cyclists are the 1:200,000 Touring Club Italiano (TCI) regional map of Umbria e Marche, or the same-scale Michelin Umbria/Marche map #359.

For walkers and mountain bikers, use the three 1:50,000 sheets covering the mountainous zones of the Marche produced by Kompass Fleischmann:

- Sheet 664: Gubbio-Fabriano
- Sheet 665: Assisi-Camerino
- Sheet 666: Monti Sibillini

Italian Tourist Office Abroad:

The Italian State Tourist Board has branches in most capital cities offering a wealth of free tourist literature. These include:

- **Chicago** - 500, North Michigan Avenue 506, Chicago IL 60611
- **London** - 1 Princes Street, London W1R 8AY.
- **Los Angeles** - Suite 550, 12400 Wilshire Blvd, Los Angeles, CA 90025
- **New York** - Suite 1565, 630 Fifth Avenue, New York NY 10111
- **Paris** - 23 rue de la Paix, 75002 Paris.
- **Sidney** - Level 4, 46 Market Street NSW 2000
- **Toronto** - Suite 503,110 Yonge Street, Toronto (Ontario) M5C 1T4

Tourist information Offices in the Marche:

For Tourist information offices just look for the italic "*i*" information symbol. Provincial capitals have offices that carry plenty of leaflets on the whole province, while other larger towns of interest to tourists will have an information office with street plans, hotel lists, etc. Smaller towns and villages often also have a *Pro Loco* office, generally only open during late afternoons. The main tourist information offices in the Marche are:

- Ancona - via Thaon de Revel, 4, 60124 Ancona. tel +39 071 358991 fax +39 071 3589929
  e-mail - iat.ancona@regione.marche.it

- Ascoli Piceno - Piazza del Popolo, 1, 63100 Ascoli Piceno. tel +39 0736 253045 fax +39 0736 252391
  e-mail: iat.ascolipiceno@regione.marche.it
- Civitanova Marche - Corso Garibaldi, 7, 62012 Civitanova Marche. tel +39 0733 813967 fax +39 0733 815027
  e-mail: iat.civitanova@regione.marche.it
- Fabriano - Corso della Repubblica, 70, 60044 Fabriano. tel +39 0732 625067 fax +39 0732 629791
  e-mail: iat.fabriano@regione.marche.it
- Fano - via C.Battisti, 10, 61032 Fano. tel +39 0721 803534 fax +39 0721 824292
  e-mail: iat.fano@regione.marche.it
- Fermo - Piazza del Popolo, 5, 63023 Fermo. tel +39 0734 228738 fax +39 0734 228325
  e-mail: iat.fermo@regione.marche.it
- Gabicce Mare - Viale della Vittoria, 41, 61011 Gabicce Mare. tel +39 0541 954424 fax +39 0541 953500
  e-mail: iat.gabicce@regione.marche.it
- Loreto - via Solari, 3, 60025 Loreto. tel +39 071 970276 fax +39 071 970020
  e-mail: iat.loreto@regione.marche.it
- Macerata - Piazza della Libertà, 12, 62100 Macerata. tel +39 0733 234807 fax +39 0733 234487
  e-mail: iat.macerata@regione.marche.it
- Pesaro - viale Trieste 164, 61100 Pesaro. tel +39 0721 69341 fax +39 0721 30462
  e-mail: iat.pesaro@regione.marche.it
- San Benedetto del Tronto - viale delle Tamerici, 5, 63039 San Benedetto del Tronto. tel +39 0735 592237 fax +39 0735 582893
  e-mail: iat.sanbenedetto@regione.marche.it
- Sarnano - Largo Ricciardi, 1, 62028 Sarnano. tel +39 0733 657144 fax +39 0733 657343
  e-mail: iat.ancona@regione.marche.it
- Senigallia - Piazzale Morandi, 2, 60019 Senigallia. tel +39 071 7922725 fax +39 071 7924930
  e-mail: iat.senigallia@regione.marche.it
- Urbino - Piazza Duca Federico, 35, 61029 Urbino. tel +39 0722 2613 fax +39 0722 2441
  e-mail: iat.urbino@regione.marche.it

Map of principal towns in the Marche

Appendix 1: Italian-English menu translator

(items with an asterisk are Marche specialities)
aceto – vinegar
affettato – sliced cured pork meats
aglio – garlic
agnello – lamb
anatra – duck
anguilla – eel
antipasto – hors d'ouvres
arrabbiata – spicy (literally "angry") pasta sauce
arrosto – roast
asparaghi – asparagus
baccalà – salt cod
basilico – basil
in bianco – "white" ie. dish without tomato
bietola – chard
bistecca (maiale/manzo) – steak (pork/ beef)
bollito – boiled
alla brace – cooked over embers
braciola – chop, usually of pork
branzino – sea bass
*****brodetto** – Marche fish stew
in brodo – in broth
*****cappelletti** – "little hats" meat-filled pasta often served in broth
*****coniglio (in porchetta)** – rabbit (stuffed with wild fennel)
contorno – vegetable dishes
*****coratella d'agnello** – fry-up of lamb's insides, tasty but not for the squeamish
costarelle – spare ribs
cotto – cooked
*****cotechino** – excellent boiled sausage
cozze – mussels
*****crescia** – see **piadina**
crostini – toasted canapes
crudo – raw
dolci – sweets
fagiano – pheasant
fagioli – beans
fagiolini – french beans
faraona – guinea fowl
farcito – stuffed
fave – broad beans
*****fegatelli** – pig's liver and bay leaves wrapped in caul fat
fegatini – chicken livers
fegato – liver
fettina – thinly sliced meat
fettuccine – pasta ribbons
fichi – figs

filetto – fillet
finocchio – fennel
manzo – beef
marmellata – jam
mela – apple
melanzane – aubergines
merluzzo – cod
miele – honey
minestra – soup, usually thinner than **zuppa**
minestrone – vegetable soup
misto – mixed
nocciole – hazelnuts
noce – walnut
nostrano, nostrale – locally produced
oca – goose
olio d'oliva – olive oil
orata – gilt-head bream
osso buco – shin of veal
ostriche – oysters
pane – bread
panforte – dried fruit spiced cake
panino – roll
panna (montata) – cream (whipped)
panzanella – salad of stale bread & tomato
pappardelle – wide pasta noodles
***passatelli** – a pasta of breadcrumbs, egg & parmesan often served in broth
patate – potatoes
penne – pasta quills
***piadina** – flat bread
***piccione (ripieno)** – (stuffed) pigeon
***stoccafisso** – dried cod (see also **baccalà**)
tacchino – turkey
***tartufo/tartufato** – truffle/flavoured with truffles
tonno – tuna
tortellini – stuffed pasta rings
triglia – red mullet
trippa – tripe
trota – trout
uovo/a – egg/s
verdura (cotta) – greens (cooked)
***vincisgrassi** – Marche version of lasagna
vitello – calf or veal
vongole – baby clams
zucchini – courgettes
zuppa – soup, usually thicker than **minestra**

Appendix 2: Notes if you're planning to move to the Marche

Buying a house

If you decide to live here, buying a home will probably be the biggest and most difficult decision you will have to make.

The best way, if you can spare the time, is to get to know an area well before deciding to buy there. Negotiate a hotel room for a long stay or rent a place, and make friends in the local bar. Remember that accommodation will cost a lot less out of season and you'll be seeing properties in a less romantic light than in high summer when anything looks great.

When it comes to buying, it is surprising how rash and unbusinesslike many foreigners become when faced with a charming but tumbledown country cottage – remember to remain detached, ask the right questions (ie. does the water supply dry up during the summer?) and, if you don't speak good Italian, have someone with you who does. As with negotions anywhere in the world, don't appear over-enthusiastic if you intend to drive a hard bargain.

Having decided that you like a property, the first stage is the signing of a *compromesso*. This *scrittura privata* or "private contract" between yourself and the seller is a legally binding document and if you change your mind you will lose whatever deposit you have paid and usually be liable to pay an additional penalty. Deposits vary but are often around 10 to 20% of the agreed purchase price.

The *compromesso* will give details of exactly what it is you are buying, including the particulars as recorded in the local *catasta*, the long-established Italian "land registry". Make sure these details are correct and correspond to what it is you *think* you are buying before you sign the document.

At a time specified in the *compromesso* the final *atto*, or contract, will be signed in front of the local *notaio*, a public official who witnesses public contracts.

Remember the *notaio* is not acting for any one of the parties – if you want to be sure that there are no nasty surprises hidden in the contract, that might, for example, give rise to neighbour problems in the future, get a local lawyer, or *avvocato*, to act for you. At this stage you will normally have to hand over the balance of the purchase price and pay any fees due to the *notaio* and estate agent, or *mediatore*.

Marche Methuselah

The secret for a long life? Living in the Marche might just be the answer according to ISTAT, Italy's national statistics office who recently announced that the region boasts the highest life expectancy in Italy, a country that already has one of the highest rates of longevity in the world. Figures for the Marche give a life expectancy of 78.8 years for men and 84.7 for women.

Restoring property

Ten ways to make life easier when doing up your dream home in the Marche (or anywhere else in Italy):

1. Always follow the official rules even if locals tell you it isn't necessary – nowadays it is; never do any work without *all* the proper permissions.
2. Don't get work done *in nero*, avoiding paying *IVA* (Italian value added tax) and not getting proper invoices. If something goes wrong, then you will have no proof of monies paid and work done; in the event of an accident on site you could even find yourself criminally responsible. For some restoration work on old properties *IVA* can be as low as 4 per cent – check with your architect whether the work is eligible for lower *IVA* rates.
3. Before you start work make sure you know exactly what you want – put as much of your ideas down on paper.
4. Don't leave any important decisions to builders and don't let builders boss you around; they love telling you that something can't be done, a common tactic when it comes to getting them to re-use old materials (of course it's always much easier for them to use nice, brand new stuff).
5. Respect local building styles and materials – some of the ugliest restorations are the result of people importing alien materials and styles from back home. Employing a good local architect should helps you avoid this pitfall – listen to what they say.
6. Don't underestimate restoration costs, particularly for old buildings; it is often much cheaper to simply demolish an old house and build a new one although the result may not be quite what you had in mind.
7. An estimate of costs or *preventivo* is essential but will probably not give you a final figure for works. Most often estimates will be given for the cost per square metre of, say, building a new roof or the cost per linear metre of putting up gutters; the final figure will be calculated at the end when the work done will be measured.
8. Remember that restoring an old house almost always involves *imprevisti* , problems that only come to light as work progresses such as walls that need serious remedial work. These *imprevisti* often substantially increase costs – make sure you agree these extra costs before the unforeseen works are carried out.
9. Check if you're property is in an earthquake zone. Much of the inland Marche is subject to earthquakes – the last was in 1997 which caused much damage around Fabriano and in neighbouring Umbria. If you are in an area prone to quakes, major restoration work will *by law* require you to carry out expensive anti-quake measures – people may suggest that you don't need to do these works but do you *really* want to be buried alive in the rubble of your dream home?
10. When drawing up your plans bear in mind just how bleak winter often is up in the mountains – a metre and a half of snow in inland areas of the region is not unheard of – and just how much central heating costs; double glazing may mean uglier windows than the pretty old ones but after a few winters here you'll understand why they are better.

Paperwork

Citizens from European Union countries will find few problems in buying property and starting a new life in Italy, and for nationals from further afield the bureaucratic hurdles needn't be too much of a barrier.

This doesn't mean, though, that you're exempt from the thorough paperwork beloved of European public officials. Foreigners frequently have an idea that anything goes in Italy and that rules are there to be ignored – in the Marche, at least, this approach all too often ends in disaster.

Citizens of EU countries and many other nationals can stay in Italy for up to three months with just a valid passport. Check with your travel agent at home to see what rules apply to your home country.

If, however, you want to live in Italy for a longer period you will at very least need to register with the Ufficio Anagrafe at your local town hall. European Union citizens no longer need a *carta di soggiorno*, and after five years residence can obtain a *soggiorno permanente* giving them effective parity with Italian citizens.

Non-EU nationals will need a *permesso di soggiorno*, or permit to stay, from the *Questura*, or main police station, in the nearest provincial capital. They will also have to answer questions concerning financial resources, property ownership, etc., and have no automatic right to stay. For the latest detailed information contact the Italian Consulate in your home country before leaving.

You will also almost certainly need to take up residency in the *comune*, or local authority district, where you decide to live, particularly if you have any plans to work here. Again for EU citizens this is straight-forward and virtually automatic. For many things, such as opening a bank account, a *certificato di residenza*, or residency certificate, is often required.

The last of the trinity of essential documents to get is your *codice fiscale*, an Italian tax code. This is one of the easiest documents to obtain, and is available from tax offices in the provincial capitals in a matter of minutes. Possession of the code does not of itself make you liable to paying Italian tax, but the number is required for numerous transaction, including property purchases.

A final tip – during your first few months carry some recent passport photos in your wallet as you never know when they may come in useful

Money matters

What follows is a brief introduction to property and income taxes and other money matters in Italy. It is by no means exhaustive – Italian tax matters are rarely straighforward and it is worth every penny of the usually modest fees to use the services of a local *commercialista*, or accountant. And be warned that the Italian love for *sigle*, or abbreviations, is given free rein when it comes to taxes.

If you are neither resident nor working here, you need only bother yourself with property taxes on any buildings that you own. Each *comune*, or town council, levies **I.M.U.** (imposta municipale unica) that is a tax on property based on size and type of property and charged to owners. At the moment there is a reduction on your principle residence. Your local *comune* also raises a separate, but relatively modest tax for refuse disposal called T.A.R.S.U. (tassa per lo smaltimento di rifiuti solidi urbani).

If you wish to work here things get rather more complicated and a *commercialista* becomes essential. And remember, even if you work for and are paid by companies abroad, if you are resident in Italy you are usually liable to pay tax here.

Italian income tax, *I.R.P.E.F.*, and national pension and health payments, paid to an authority called *I.N.P.S.*, are the two principal fiscal burdens you will have to get to grips with. If you are self-employed or have your own company you will also have to get involved with *IVA* (Italian value added tax); the very low threshold for *IVA* means that virtually anyone who is self-employed has to charge *IVA* on sales or services. At the risk of sounding repetitive, don't try any of this without a *commercialista*.

Health

Contrary to received opinion, the Italian public health service, at least in the Marche, works very well. A modern, well-run network of hospitals covers the region and you'll never be far from emergency treatment should you need it.

In the event of serious illness or injury, head for the 24-hour casualty departments (*pronto soccorso* or *punto di primo intervento*) at any hospital. For minor aches and pains make for the local *farmacia*, or dispensing chemist. They keep normal shop hours and can be spotted by a green cross outside; they also operate an emergency out-of-hours service on a shift basis, details of which are displayed in the window.

If you decide to live in the Marche you will probably want to sign up with a general practitioner (*medico di famiglia*) through the local A.S.L. – Azienda Sanitaria Locale – office and if you are earning you'll have to pay your regular national insurance contributions (INPS in Italian). You can, of course, always consult a doctor as a paying private patient without getting involved with the A.S.L.

Under the public health system, unless you are elderly or chronically ill, you'll have to contribute towards prescriptions and hospital out-patient treatment, known as a *"ticket"* (yes, in English).

Dental treatment in the Marche, as in the rest of Italy, is generally excellent but expensive, and is not covered by the public health service.

Index

place names in **bold**
accommodation notes; 128
Acquacanina; 68
Acqualagna; 18; 48
Albornoz, Cardinal; 24
Amandola; 70
Ancona; 82
   airport; 126
   Cathedral of San Ciriaco; 82
   Colle Guasco; 82
   Fontana del Calamo; 83
   Loggia dei Mercanti; 83
   Mole Vanvitelliana; 82
   Museo Archeologico delle Marche; 83
   Piazza del Plebiscito; 83
   Pinacoteca; 83
   San Domenico, Church of; 83
   Sant'Agostino; 83
   Santa Maria della Piazza, Church of; 83
   Teatro delle Muse; 83
   Trajan's Arch; 82
antique fairs; 37
Apecchio; 109
Apiro; 56
Appignano del Tronto; 72
Arcevia; 52
Ascoli Piceno; 84
   caffè Miletti; 84
   Duomo; 84
   Palazzo del Popolo; 84
   Piazza Arringo; 84
   Piazza del Popolo; 84
   Pinacoteca Civica art gallery; 84

   Quintana tournament; 85
   San Francesco, Church of; 84
Badia di San Pietro; 64
Balzo di Montegallo; 70
Bandiere Arancioni awards; 88
banks, opening hours; 131
Barbara; 52
Belisarius, Byzantine general; 22
Belvedere Ostrense; 57
Blue Flag awards; 80
Bocca Serriola. *see* Serriola Pass
Bolognola; 68
brodetto fish stew; 112
Bronzi Dorati. *see* Gilded Bronzes
Buonaccorsi, gardens; 65
bus services; 127
buying property; 138
Byzantine style; 27
Cagli; 85
calcioni; 116
Caldarola; 61; **86**
Camerino; 61; **87**
Cantiano; 48
Carlo Crivelli; 30; **31**; 72
Carpegna; 43; 44
Cartoceto; 47
Castelfidardo; 65
   battle of; 25
Castello della Rancia; 62
Castello di Montefiore; 66
Castelluccio; 69
Castelraimondo; 61
Castelsantangelo sul Nera; 69

144

Chiaravalle, Abbey of; 57
ciauscolo; 15
cicerchia; 55
Cingoli; 56; **88**
Civitanova Marche; 78
clothing; 130
Conero Regional Park; 103
Corinaldo; 52; **89**
Corridonia; 59
Cossignano; 72
Crivelli, Carlo; 73; 84
Cupra Marittima; 79
Cupramontana; 56
currency; 131
Da Varano family; 87
driving in the Marche; 127
emergency medical help; 131
erbe del campo; 14
events in the Marche; 35
Exarchate of Ravenna; 22
Fabriano; **90**
    paper; 90
Falerio Picenus; 73
Falerone; 73
Fano; 78; **91**
Federico da Montefeltro; 121
Fermignano; 45
Fermo; 73; **92**
Fiastra Abbey; 59
Fiastra Lake; 68
Filottrano; 66
Flaminian Way. *see* Via Flaminia
Fonte Avellana, monastery; 50
food in the Marche; 14

food shopping; 16
food translator; 136
Force; 74
formaggio di fossa; 43
Fossombrone; 47; **93**
Francesca da Rimini; 97
Francesco di Giorgio Martini; 29; 45
Frasassi Caves; 52; **94**
Frederick II, Emperor; 23; 98
Frontone; 51
Furlo Gorge; 22; 47; **95**
Gabicce Mare; 77; **96**
Gagliole; 61
Genga; 53
Gentile da Fabriano; 27
Gigli, Beniamino; 110
Gilded Bronzes, Pergola; 106
Giovanni Bellini; 30
Giovanni Santi; 85
Gola dell'Infernaccio; 70
gothic style; 27
Gradara, Castle; 96; 108
Grottammare; 79
Gubbio; 48
guelphs & ghibellines; 23
Helvia Ricina; 62; 101
holidays, national; 129
Holy House, legend of; 100
Holy Roman Empire; 22
i vlurd; 104
Infernaccio Gorge; 116
International Gothic style; 27
internet; 132

145

Italian League; 24
Jesi; 55; **97**
Lace, Offida; 104
Lacrima di Morro d'Alba, wine; 57
Lago di Pilato; **70**; 116
Leopardi, Giacomo; 110; 123
life expectancy in the Marche; 138
Lorenzo Lotto; 30; **31**; 72; 88; 110
Loreto; 65; **99**
Loro Piceno; 60
Luca Signorelli; 30
Macerata; **100**
   open-air opera festival; 35
   Sferisterio; 101
Macerata Feltria; 44
Macereto, Sanctuary of; 69
Macereto, Sanctuary of; 123
Madonna dell'Ambro; 70
Maiolati Spontini; 56
mannerism; 29
Marche wines; 19
Massa Fermana; 73
Matelica; 56
Meletti, *digestivo*; 20
Melozzo da Forlì; 30
menu, typical Marche; 15
mistrà, digestivo; 20
mobile phones; 132
Mogliano; 73
Mondavio; 52
Montalto delle Marche; 74
Montappone; 73
Monte Catria; 50
Monte Conero; 63; **102**

Monte Petrano; 86
Monte San Bartolo park; 97
Monte San Giusto; 59
Monte Vettore; 34; 69; 116
Monte Vidon Corrado; 73
Montecarotto; 56
Montecassiano; 66
Montedinove; 74
Montefano; 66
Montefiore dell'Aso; 72
Montefortino; 70
Montegranaro; 59
Montelparo; 74
Montelupone; 65
Montemaggiore al Metauro; 47
Montemonaco; 70
Monterubbiano; 72
Monti Sibillini Natural Park; 117
Moresco; 72
Morro D'Alba; 57
Napoleon Bonaparte; 24
Narses, Byzantine general; 22
Numana; 64; 78; 102
Offagna; 66
Offida; 72; **103**
olive ascolane; 15; 84
opening times; 12
Osimo; 65; **105**
Ostra; 57
Ostra Vetere; 52
Parco Naturale dei Monti Sibillini. *see* Monti Sibillini Natural Park
passatelli; 15
Pedaso; 79

146

Pergola; 51; **106**
Pergolesi, Giovanni Battista; 98
Pesaro; 77; **107**
Petriolo; 59
piadina; 15
Piano Grande; 34; 67; 69; 116
Piceni; 21
Piero della Francesca; 29; **32**; 120
Pietrarubbia; 44
Pietro da Rimini; 30
Pieve Torina; 69
Pievebovigliana; 68
Piobbico; 109
Poggio di Bretta; 72
Pollenza; 62
Pontericcioli; 48
pork specialities; 16
Porto Potenza Picena; 78
Porto Recanati; 78
Porto San Giorgio; 78
Porto Sant'Elpidio; 78
Portonovo; 64; 78; 102
post offices; 132
Potenza Picena; 65
Quintana tournament; 85
Raphael; 30; **32**; 120
Recanati; 65; **109**
religious events; 39
renaissance style; 27
restoring property; 139
Ripatransone; 72
romanesque style; 27
Rossini Opera Festival; 35
Rossino, Gioachino; 107

Rosso Conero, wine; 19; 66; 103
sagre; 36
Saint Thomas Becket; 74
Salimbeni brothers; 122
Saltara; 47
Salvi, Giovan Battista. *see* Sassoferrato, Il
San Benedetto del Tronto; 79; **111**
San Claudio al Chienti; 58
San Ginesio; 60
San Lorenzo in Campo; 51
San Severino Marche; 61
San Vittore delle Chiuse; 95
San Vittore delle Chiuse, church of; 52
Sant'Angelo in Vado; **112**
Sant'Elpidio a Mare; 59
Santa Maria a Piè di Chienti; 59
Santa Vittoria in Matenano; 73
sapa; 20
Sarnano; 68; **113**
Sassi Simone and **Simoncello**; 44
Sasso Tetto; 68; 114
Sassocorvaro; 43
Sassoferrato; 50
Sassoferrato, Il; 50
Senigallia; 78; **114**
Sentinum; 50
Sentinum, battle of; 26
Serra de' Conti; 57
Serra San Quirico; **115**
Serra Sant'Abbondio; 50
Serrapetrona; 61
Serriola Pass; 109
Servigliano; 73

Sibillini Mountains; 67; **116**
Simone De Magistris; 86; 123
Sirolo; 64; 78; 102
spa towns; 114
Spontini, Gaspare; 56
St Joseph of Copertino; 105
St Maria Goretti; 89
St Nicholas of Tolentino; 118
Staffolo; 55
taxis; 126
telephones; 132
Tempio del Valadier, Frassasi; 95
Theodoric, king; 22
tipping; 130
Tolentino; 24; 62; **117**
Totila, Gothic king; 22
tourist information offices; 133
trains in Le Marche; 126
travel documents; 130
Treia; 62
truffles; 18
   cultivation of; 113
Uccello, Paolo; 29
Umbri; 21
Urbania; **118**

Urbino; 44; **119**
  Egyptian obelisk; 121
  Museo Archeologico; 120
  Oratorio di San Giovanni Battista; 122
  Palazzo Ducale; 120
  San Bernadino, Church of; 122
Urbisaglia; 60
Urbs Salvia; 60
Ussita; 69
Varnelli, *digestivo*; 20
Venarotta; 74
Verdicchio; 19; 54
Via Flaminia; 21; 26; 46; 95
Villa Potenza; 62; 66
vincisgrassi; 61
vino cotto; 20
vino santo; 20
visner, wild cherry liqueur; 20
Visso; 69; **122**
vitalba; 14
Vittore Crivelli; 31
weather; 129
when to visit; 11